Proficiency PASSKEY

Student's Book

NICK KENNY

MACMILLAN
HEINEMANN
English Language Teaching

Contents Map

Introduction

This book is designed to help you prepare for all aspects of the Proficiency examination. Each unit in the book includes a wide variety of tasks and exercises, all designed to help you to develop your vocabulary and practise the reading, writing, listening and speaking skills you need to pass the examination.

There are Help Sections throughout the book which give advice and practice in dealing with each type of question you will have to answer in the examination and further practice of the Use of English exercises can be found in the Exam Practice Section at the end of each unit.

The separate workbook provides lots of further practice in the areas of grammar, vocabulary and writing skills, as well as giving the opportunity for further practice of the exam-style tasks and exercises.

Below is a description of the Proficiency examination. More information is available in the workbook. I hope you enjoy using this book and that you are successful in the examination.

The Certificate of Proficiency in English

The Proficiency examination is taken by people in over 70 countries all over the world. It is the highest level examination in English as a Foreign Language offered by the University of Cambridge.

The examination has five papers. They can be summarized as follows:

Paper 1   Reading Comprehension (1 hour)

This paper is divided into two sections. The first section tests your knowledge of vocabulary, collocation and other aspects of usage through multiple-choice gap-fill questions. Examples of these questions can be found at the beginning of each Exam Practice section in this book.

The second section tests comprehension of gist, content, tone and register in passages of written English. There are three texts of between 350 and 550 words in length, with around five multiple-choice questions on each. There are examples of these questions on reading texts throughout the book.

Paper 2   Composition (2 hours)

In this paper you have to write two compositions of between 300 and 350 words from a choice of five.

Examiners who mark the compositions give credit for good organization, task fulfilment, and the quality and range of language used. Examples of marked compositions can be found on pages 201–203.

Paper 3   Use of English (2 hours)

This paper tests your knowledge and control of the English language. There are two sections. Section A is divided into four parts.

- Cloze passage. There is a Help section on pages 27–29 and examples of this task in every unit of the book.
- Sentence transformations. There is a Help section on pages 75–77.
- Key word transformations. There is a Help section on pages 116–117.
- Gap-fill sentences. There is a Help section on page 156.

Section B contains a passage of around 550-650 words followed by comprehension questions. There are examples of these questions on reading texts throughout the book.

A final task in this section is to write a summary, based on one aspect of the argument put forward in the passage. There is a Help with Summary writing section on page 126.

Paper 4   Listening

This paper tests your understanding of three or four listening texts which are played on a cassette tape. The texts are around three minutes long and you hear each one twice. There are a total of 25–30 questions. Questions are likely to include:

- multiple-choice questions
- note completion and sentence completion tasks
- true/false and matching tasks

There are Help with Listening sections on pages 16–17 and 34 and examples of all these task types on listening texts throughout the book.

Paper 5   Speaking (15 minutes approximately)

This paper tests your ability to discuss and comment on issues and express opinions. There are three main parts to the test around a central theme.

- Describing and comparing a set of thematically linked photographs. There is a Help section on pages 46–47 and many opportunities to practise this throughout the book.
- To comment on a short reading passage related to the theme. There is a Help section on pages 92–93 and many opportunities to practise this throughout the book.
- To take part in a broader discussion related to the theme. There are many opportunities to practise such tasks throughout the book.

Sign of the Times

SPEAKING 1
Expressing opinions

1 Talk to your partner about

your favourite food:
* why you like it
* when you like to eat it
* how it should be prepared

the importance of these things in food.

taste	colour	texture
smell	temperature	presentation

2 Some visitors from overseas are coming to visit your area for a day and want to find out about the local cuisine. What would you recommend they eat? Talk about:

restaurants	breakfast
snacks	bars
lunch	drinks
dinner	home cooking

3 What do these terms mean?
   a convenience food
   b fast food
   c health food

4 What do you think of these types of food?

Comprehension

■ **1** Look at this headline. What do you think the article is going to be about?

■ **2** Read quickly to find out what happened in each of these years or decades.

| 1880s | 1904 | 1921 | 1950s | 1960s | 1970s | 1980s | 1990s |

Crisis in a Sesame Bun

DESPITE THE BAD publicity surrounding 'Mad Cow Disease' in the 1990s, the hamburger remains an icon for the twentieth century. In its provenance, preparation, purchase and very place of consumption it tells in microcosm the history of the century. In each decade its character and its image subtly reflected the shifting fashions and preoccupations of the era.

10 Its origins are cloaked in an uncertainty that only assists its status as a characterless object to which each generation may add whatever relish it chooses. Its connections with the German city of Hamburg are unclear. Although every culinary civilization has had some form of ground meat patty, most food historians do accept a link with the eponymous Baltic port.

Thus the hamburger enters history as the
20 plain but honest food of poor but ambitious immigrants to the United States. Indeed according to one food expert it had its origins in the fare of a German-owned shipping line on whose vessels in the 1880s, Hamburg beef was minced and then mixed with breadcrumbs, eggs and onions and served with bread.

But it was at the World Fair in St Louis in 1904 that it first became a symbol of mass-
30 produced cuisine. It was there that the bun was first introduced and the result was wildly popular. Soon after, in 1921, the first hamburger chain was established. But generally the burger remained a wholesome home-made dish. Older Americans still cherish childhood memories of Mom grinding good fresh steak and, after adding onion and seasoning, taking the result straight out to the charcoal grill in the

40 garden, but like all things American when exported it has been debased and perverted.

The hamburger first entered British consciousness as part of the post-second world war spending spree, when beef became a symbol of the new prosperity. When in the late 1950s the frozen beefburger was introduced (renamed to avoid unnecessary questions about why it did not taste of ham) the thin little cake of bland rubbery meat was
50 a glamour product. It was somehow foreign and, of course, frozen, which was then the height of new technology. It was the first of the new range of 'convenience' foods which were about to make the world a better place and begin the liberation of women from the drudgery of home-cooking and housework. The older generation did not approve, which made it all the better. In the Sixties the hamburger was a symbol of the techno age –
60 perfectly circular and streamlined. It was as uniform and relentlessly predictable as only the latest technology could make it.

True, there were those who rebelled against it, but to most the hamburger was a reflection of the national love affair with Americana. It was a phenomenon which was made flesh in Seventies London with the trendy burgers of the Great American Disaster and the Hard Rock Café, and in
70 many other cities round the world.

In the Eighties another subtle shift occurred. People became aware that America was no longer another place but a culture which had spread throughout the world. And the hamburger became globalized, too, in the form of McDonald's. With its US home market, like the fat in its burgers, heavily saturated, McDonald's looked abroad. By the

end of the Eighties it had
grown to such a size that
every day 28 million global
citizens ate there and the Big
Mac became omnipresent.

McDonald's stormed the
world, but its successes also
drew upon it in the Nineties
the criticisms which were
levelled at that era. Food
experts began to see the
world's changing culinary
tastes as a symbol of what is
wrong with the new
consumerism. 'The ham-
burger is a metaphor for our
times – cheap, convenient
and an indication that we
have given up any real
interest in what we eat,' said
the leading food writer
Frances Bissell, lamenting
the trends of our increasingly
obese society towards
snacking on the hoof or
before the TV instead of
eating proper meals.

Then along came 'Mad Cow
Disease' and even though the
average person was told they
had more chance of winning
the National Lottery than
contracting 'Mad Person
Disease', with it came the
dreadful realization that the
cheap, convenient, easy way
out might, in the end, turn
out to be none of these
things.

3 Now read the article again and answer these questions.

1 Explain in your own words what is meant by the phrase 'the hamburger remains an icon for the twentieth century'. (lines 3–4)

2 In your own words, explain why the writer regards the hamburger as an essentially 'characterless' object.

3 What is referred to by the phrase 'the eponymous Baltic port'? (line 18)

4 What is the 'result' referred to in line 31?

5 In what way has the hamburger been 'debased and perverted'? (line 41)

6 What is a 'spending spree'? (line 44)

7 Explain in your own words why the hamburger was renamed 'beefburger' in Britain in the 1950s.

8 What is meant in this context by the phrase 'a glamour product'? (line 50)

9 Why is the word 'convenience' in line 53 in quotation marks?

10 What do you understand about the writer's view of Britain from the phrase 'the national love affair with Americana'? (lines 65–66)

11 Why did *McDonald's* decide to open branches outside the USA?

12 What is meant by the phrase 'snacking on the hoof'? (line 103) Why is this phrase particularly appropriate to the article?

13 Why does the author compare 'Mad Person Disease' with winning the National Lottery?

4 In the exam it is important to answer the comprehension questions in the correct way. Look back at your answers to questions 1–13.

Have you written a complete sentence for each answer?

Does your sentence answer the question completely?

Have you used your own words?

Look at these three answers to question 13. Which is best? Why?

a *Because they are similar.*

b *The author wants to show that people are very unlikely to contract 'Mad Person Disease'.*

c *The average person was told they had more chance of winning the National Lottery than contracting 'Mad Person Disease'.*

When answering comprehension questions, REMEMBER to:
- use complete sentences;
- use your own words;
- explain exactly what you mean.

VOCABULARY 1
Definitions

■ 1 Choose the best definition **A**, **B** or **C** for each of these words from the article.

1 provenance (line 4)
A range of ingredients **B** place of origin **C** number of varieties

2 preoccupations (line 9)
A special developments **B** recurrent problems **C** particular interests

3 fare (line 23)
A food provided **B** price of the ticket **C** type of journey

4 wholesome (line 34)
A traditional **B** ordinary **C** healthy

5 cherish (line 36)
A value **B** confess to **C** mention

6 bland (line 49)
A soft textured **B** lacking in taste **C** pale coloured

7 drudgery (line 56)
A loneliness **B** long hours **C** dull work

8 omnipresent (line 83)
A well-regarded **B** reasonably priced **C** found everywhere

9 lamenting (line 100)
A criticising **B** regretting **C** describing

10 obese (line 102)
A overstressed **B** overworked **C** overweight

WRITING 1
Summary

■ 1 Look at this phrase from the article.

'it tells in microcosm the history of the century'

What do you understand by the term 'microcosm'?

■ 2 In your own words, explain how the hamburger changed to suit the fashions of different periods of the twentieth century. Write no more than 100 words.

Use the questions below to help you structure your summary.

1 What do we know about the hamburger at the beginning of the century?

2 What important thing started in the 1920s?

3 What made hamburgers popular in Britain in the 1950s, 1960s and 1970s?

4 What did hamburgers come to symbolize in the 1980s and 1990s?

How will you link the ideas together? Look at the words and phrases in the box. Can you use any of these in your summary?

first	later	originally	more recently	when
before	at first	after that	since	

GRAMMAR 1
Review of past tenses

1

1   Look at the article on pages 2 and 3 again. For each paragraph, look through quickly and decide what tense most of the main verbs are in (e.g. simple present, past simple, present perfect, etc.). Why is each tense appropriate to each paragraph?

2   Find some examples of the present perfect and past perfect tenses in the article. Underline them.

Why has this tense been used in each case?

2   Put the verbs in brackets into the correct tense (present simple, present perfect, simple past, or past perfect).

The name hamburger (**1**) _____ (date) back to German immigrants travelling to the USA in the 1880s. It's only since 1902, however, that hamburgers (**2**) _____ (serve) in a bun. Before the 1920s, when the first chain of hamburger restaurants (**3**) _____ (open), most hamburgers (**4**) _____ (cook) at home.

The fashion for hamburgers in Britain (**5**) _____ (start) in the 1950s, and by the 1970s hamburger restaurants (**6**) _____ (become) some of the most fashionable in London. In the 1980s, *McDonald's* (**7**) _____ (decide) to expand their operations outside the USA and by the 1990s they (**8**) _____ (open) restaurants in most countries in the world.

Since 1980, people (**9**) _____ (begin) to question the assumption that fast food, and hamburgers in particular, (**10**) _____ (represent) progress.

📖 N.B. The Workbook has further work on past tenses.

PHRASAL VERBS 1

1   Look at this extract from the article. Underline the phrasal verb in the extract.

'with it came the realization that the cheap, convenient, easy way out might turn out to be none of these things'.

2   Complete each sentence with a suitable verb.

1   Guests leaving the hotel are asked to _____ out of the hotel before 11 o'clock in the morning.

2   The investigation into the causes of the accident will be _____ out by a team of experts.

3   A foot injury has forced Fred to _____ out of Saturday's race.

4   The address was very badly printed and I couldn't _____ out the street name.

5   She went to the dentist's to have a tooth _____ out.

6   Reading comprehension questions should be _____ out in full.

📖 N.B. The Workbook has further examples of phrasal verbs with *out*.

SPEAKING 2
Talking about photographs

1 Decide who is Student A and who is Student B and look at one of the two pictures labelled **A** or **B**.

Tell your partner about your picture. Try to use words and phrases you have learnt from the article about hamburgers. Talk about:

- the people; what they are doing and why; how they are feeling

- how you feel about the picture

- the images presented in the picture

A

B

2 You have been asked to help design a poster on the theme 'Icons of the twentieth century' which will symbolize 20th century life. The poster will feature three pictures; one of a hamburger plus two others.

1 Look at these images and talk about how suitable each would be for the poster. Discuss your choices in relation to the following areas:

- the century as a whole
- people all round the world
- the future

Think about the positive and negative aspects of your choices.

2 Agree on the two images you want to put on the poster with the hamburger and then write a short report explaining your decision. (100 words)

Cloze passage

Fill each of the numbered blanks in the passage with **one** suitable word from the box. The first one has been done for you as an example.

although	however	which	whose	why	there	at
most	come	go	use	had	round	per
for	up	in	out	away	far	~~been~~

Trolley Tales

Raymond Joseph of Strasbourg, is believed to have (**0**) *been* the inventor of the modern 4-wheeled wire supermarket trolley, (**1**) _____ first arrived in Britain in 1950, at a shop in South London. (**2**) _____ are now 1,300,000 active nationally, and (**3**) _____ 15 million shoppers safely manoeuvre a trolley (**4**) _____ their local supermarket each week, maybe it shouldn't (**5**) _____ as a surprise to learn that accidents do happen.

There are, in fact, 7000 trolley-related injuries (**6**) _____ year and three people were actually imprisoned last year (**7**) _____ trolley offences; one man after a ramming incident that followed an attempt (**8**) _____ trolley-queue jumping and another who punched a fellow shopper (**9**) _____ trolley had Achilles-heeled his wife.

But the (**10**) _____ revealing statistic concerning trolleys is that each year 140,000 of them (**11**) _____ missing. They mostly turn (**12**) _____ leaning against lampposts or rusting semi-submerged in rivers, indeed 7000 were dragged (**13**) _____ of the River Thames alone last year. But others are (**14**) _____ from abandoned, finding (**15**) _____ as parrot cages, plant stands, barbecue grills or tool containers. It's not always absolutely clear (**16**) _____ some people take them, (**17**) _____ . Police once visited an 82-year-old woman's flat and took (**18**) _____ 41 shopping trolleys she (**19**) _____ bought home and stored (**20**) _____ her lounge. 'I'm so glad they're going,' she said.

⌨ LISTENING 1
Part One
Matching

1 Before you listen discuss these questions with your partner.

1 What is the attitude towards cigarette smoking in your country? Is this attitude changing?

2 Where is it possible to buy cigarettes:
- in your country?
- in any other countries you know about?

3 Do you think the sale of cigarettes should be restricted? Talk about:
- age of buyers
- places where they are sold
- price controls
- level of tax imposed on them

2 You will hear part of a radio discussion about supermarkets selling cut-price cigarettes. For questions **1–9** decide which of the two speakers makes each point. Write:

        J = if only Joanne makes this point

OR **N** = if only Nigel makes this point

OR **B** = if both Nigel and Joanne make this point

1 There is little doubt about the harmful effects of smoking.   **1** ☐

2 Supermarkets are setting a bad example to the young.   **2** ☐

3 Supermarkets have a hypocritical attitude.   **3** ☐

4 The price of cigarettes affects how easy people find it to give up smoking.   **4** ☐

5 More people will start smoking if cigarettes are cheap.   **5** ☐

6 Supermarkets are using cheap cigarettes to attract new customers.   **6** ☐

7 Poor people often spend a lot of their money on cigarettes.   **7** ☐

8 Supermarkets should consider giving up the sale of all cigarettes.   **8** ☐

9 Supermarkets seem to regard smoking as an equivalent risk to eating unhealthy foods.   **9** ☐

Part Two

1 Look at these phrases from the listening text. Some words or short phrases have been removed. Look quickly to see if you can remember or guess the missing words or phrases.

This is one of the (**1**) _____ biggest preventable causes of death.

That (**2**) _____ is inconsistent with promoting a cheap cigarette.

They (**3**) _____ have a leaflet warning of the dangers of smoking.

It's the (**4**) _____ biggest factor that encourages smokers to increase their intake.

They are (**5**) _____ big chains that they can (**6**) _____ afford to sell their cigarettes (**7**) _____ more cheaply.

If supermarkets are (**8**) _____ interested in health, they should be reviewing the (**9**) _____ question of whether they sell tobacco products (**10**) _____ .

There's (**11**) _____ as a safe level of cigarette smoking.

Now listen again to check for the missing words.

VOCABULARY 2
Prefixes

■ **1** Look at these phrases from the listening text. What type of words have been underlined?

This has <u>enraged</u> health campaigners.
It <u>encourages</u> smokers to increase their intake.
It's the factor that will <u>enable</u> adolescents to take up smoking.

■ **2** Complete each sentence with a word from the box and the prefix *en*.

circle	close	danger	sure	roll	visage
force	lighten	rich	list	joy	large

1 To get your copy of the report, please write _____ a stamped, addressed envelope.

2 Laws aimed at preventing young people from taking up smoking are very difficult to _____ .

3 The old town is now _____ by a ring of modern suburbs.

4 The supermarket is being _____ and will soon have a super new bakery and delicatessen.

5 I'm going to _____ on a course to learn word-processing skills.

6 I'd like supermarkets to _____ that young people are not tempted to buy cigarettes there.

7 I can't _____ a meal in a restaurant where people are allowed to smoke.

8 I wonder if I could _____ your support in an anti-smoking campaign.

9 The plain meat sauce can be _____ with herbs and spices if you prefer.

10 People who smoke actually _____ the lives of themselves and others.

11 Do you _____ any problems in convincing the supermarkets to change their policies?

12 I don't seem to have understood so far, I wonder if you could _____ me?

SPEAKING 3
Expressing opinions

■ **1** Do you think that smoking should be banned in certain places?

Talk to your partner about:

- public transport
- places of entertainment
- schools and colleges
- eating places
- other public places

WRITING 2
Articles

1 You've been asked to write an article for a young people's magazine. The title of the article is 'Changing Attitudes to Smoking'.

1 Look at these three plans. Which one would you choose for your article? Why? Would you make any changes to the one you've chosen?

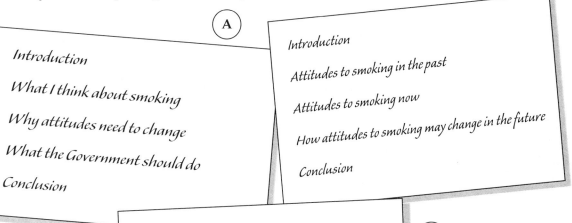

A

Introduction

What I think about smoking

Why attitudes need to change

What the Government should do

Conclusion

B

Introduction

Attitudes to smoking in the past

Attitudes to smoking now

How attitudes to smoking may change in the future

Conclusion

C

Introduction

Why attitudes to smoking are changing

How attitudes to smoking are changing

Results of changing attitudes to smoking

Conclusion

2 Find a partner who has chosen the same plan as you. Together make a list of points to include in each of the paragraphs.

3 Write the introduction to the article. How long should it be? What should it contain?

4 What will be the main tense of each paragraph? Will any verbs be in other tenses? Look back at page 5.

2 Look at the words and phrases in the box. Most of them are used in written English when we are making lists of points or adding information when building up an argument. But, which one would you use to:

- make a contrast
- draw a conclusion?

| to begin with | moreover | however | furthermore | what's more |
| likewise | secondly | therefore | in addition | |

3 Now write paragraphs using your notes from above. Try to use some of the linking words from the box where appropriate.

📖 N. B. The Workbook has further work on linking words.

READING 2
Multiple choice

■ **1** Before you read the article discuss these questions with your partner.

1 Why are people frightened of going to the dentist?

2 Talk about a good or bad experience you, or someone you know, has had at the dentist.

3 What is a phobia? What sort of things do people have phobias about? How common do you think dental phobia is?

4 What advice would you give someone who is afraid of going to the dentist?

■ **2** Read the article about dental phobia.

AFRAID TO OPEN WIDE

RECENT RESEARCH carried out by dentists and psychiatrists has shown that fear of the dentist is listed fifth among commonly held fears in many countries. Although figures are
10 **not available, some degree of dental phobia is estimated to affect about 30% of all adults, with many unable even to entertain the idea of dental work being done under anaesthetic.**

20 As with most forms of phobic behaviour, the origins of dental fear tends to be found in childhood or adolescence. A traumatic dental experience is generally central, possibly with a critical or inconsiderate dentist, or maybe backed up by unfavourable experiences related by others, especially family members. Such experiences can influence adult behaviour despite any amount of educational and media coverage to the contrary.

The consequences of dental phobia can be traumatic in themselves. Over many years, a condition which is treatable
30 can deteriorate into one which is not. Phobic patients are highly likely to suffer from dental disease and end up slowly losing their teeth or in emergency services.

When Clare Lodge was eleven, she visited a dentist who decided to do about twelve fillings in one session. 'I had to have a lot of injections, was enormously frightened and in pain for days and days afterwards,' she recalls. 'I was a dental phobic for years after that. Although I was still young enough to be forced to go, I refused to have injections because they had become associated with pain.
40 When I was older I stopped going to the dentist for good.'

'I was very lucky – I didn't have many problems with my teeth; but recently I realized I had broken a tooth and really needed a filling.'

Ms Lodge, a training consultant, eventually got help – from a new dental service called *Feelgood Dentistry* which provides psychotherapy for dental phobics. 'I have to say I was sceptical at first,' she says, 'the therapist made me play back the scene when I was eleven in my mind – but as though I was sitting in the cinema and watching it on the
50 screen. He told me to imagine the picture getting smaller and smaller, and in black and white. Then he asked me to play the film backwards – so that the last thing that happened was the injection coming out of my mouth'.

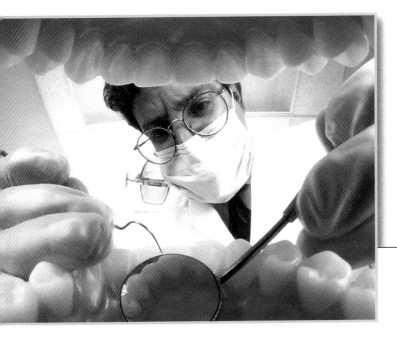

Feelgood Dentistry is a group of professionals with a
particular interest in helping dental phobics, by
providing them with psychotherapy services. They have
discovered a 'talking cure', that is an effective and
friendly form of treatment, often producing dramatic
results. Graduated, controlled exposure of patients to
60 the feared stimulus is the guiding principal behind
treatment. Like Clare Lodge, the patient first has a
session, in a room near the surgery, with a
psychotherapist who will work with them to help them
leave their fear in the past. They will then have a
consultation with the dentist. Psychotherapy is more
effective if patients go immediately into the surgery,
even if only for a consultation, rather than waiting
several weeks.

The group also hopes to demystify the dentist and his
70 equipment. All dentists do not cause pain. Clare Lodge
had not been to the dentist's in eighteen years when she
went to *Feelgood Dentistry*. 'It put everything into
perspective,' she says. 'The therapist made me appreciate
that what I'd gone through as a youngster was not a
huge drama; simply an insignificant moment in my life.
On that occasion when I was a child, that particular
dentist caused me pain. This does not mean to say that
my childhood experience will be repeated.'

'When I finally underwent dental treatment, the original
80 nightmare situation was back in history. I felt on top of
the situation. It wasn't completely pain-free, but it was
manageable. Until that point, the idea of ever seeing
another dentist had been a major ordeal, one that I felt I
could never put myself through again.'

3 Now answer the questions **1–5**.
Choose the answer, **A**, **B**, **C** or **D**
which you think fits best.

1 Most dental phobias can be
accounted for by

 A bad personal experiences.
 B stories told by friends or family.
 C scenes from films or TV
 programmes.
 D the attitude of certain dentists.

2 In the years immediately
following her dental trauma,
Clare Lodge

 A refused to go back to the
 dentist at all.
 B only went to the dentist when
 she was in pain.
 C was fortunate enough not to
 need dental treatment.
 D had no choice but to continue
 going to the dentist.

3 Clare says that when she first
went to *Feelgood Dentistry* she felt

 A embarrassed that it was
 necessary.
 B defensive about her problem.
 C doubtful about their methods.
 D reluctant to talk about her
 problem.

4 How does the *Feelgood Dentistry*
group help phobics?

 A The dentists are trained as
 psychotherapists.
 B The dental treatment takes
 place gradually, over time.
 C A psychotherapist is present
 during the dental treatment.
 D Patients overcome their fears
 before having dental treatment.

5 What does Clare say about the
dental treatment she eventually
had?

 A It was painless.
 B She still felt frightened.
 C She felt she was in control.
 D It was an ordeal.

4 Look at these pairs of words and decide what difference in meaning, if any, there is between them.

1	**a** anaesthetic		7	**a** associated	
	b painkiller			**b** connected	
2	**a** adolescence		8	**a** sceptical	
	b childhood			**b** cynical	
3	**a** traumatic		9	**a** psychotherapist	
	b upsetting			**b** psychiatrist	
4	**a** inconsiderate		10	**a** demystify	
	b tactless			**b** clarify	
5	**a** consequences		11	**a** injections	
	b results			**b** inoculations	
6	**a** deteriorate		12	**a** treatable	
	b improve			**b** curable	

PRONUNCIATION
Word stress

1 Look at the words in the box. Underline the stressed syllable in each one.

anaesthetic	adolescence	traumatic	inconsiderate
consequences	deteriorate	injections	associated
sceptical	psychotherapy	psychiatrist	demystify

2 Listen to check and compare your pronunciation of these words with that on the tape. If you find these words difficult to pronounce, practise saying them with your partner.

VOCABULARY 3
Prepositions

Complete each sentence with a suitable preposition. Then look back at the article on pages 12 and 13 to check.

1 Research has been carried _____ by psychiatrists.

2 Dental work is often done _____ local anaesthetic.

3 The consequences _____ dental phobia can be traumatic.

4 A treatable condition can deteriorate _____ one which is not.

5 Clare was _____ pain for days after her treatment.

6 Phobic patients are likely to suffer _____ dental disease.

7 *Feelgood Dentistry* has a particular interest _____ helping phobics.

8 *Feelgood Dentistry* provides phobics _____ a cure.

9 Patients have a consultation _____ a dentist.

10 Clare says the treatment put everything _____ perspective.

GRAMMAR 2
Causatives

1 Look at these phrases:

She went to the dentist to have a tooth filled.
Her teeth are not straight, so she'll have to have a brace fitted.

What grammatical form is common to them? When do we use this form?

2 Look at the words connected with the dentist. How many of them can be used with this form? Write some example sentences.

drill	fill	brace	take out/extract	decay
chair	X-ray	bib	crown	plate
check-up	injection	polish	hygiene	

📖 N.B. The Workbook has further work on causatives.

WRITING 3
Describing an event

Describe the experience of going to the dentist for a check-up from when you arrive to when you leave. Begin your description with the words.

When you go to the dentist, the first thing …

Who is *you* in this sentence?
Which tense will you use? Why?

Think about:
- what you do on arrival/the waiting room
- when you are called/the dentist's room as you walk in
- where you sit/what you can see from there
- the dentist/what the dentist says/does
- what you have to do
- how you feel before/during/afterwards

At the dentist's

Receptionist
Waiting Room – chair
                magazines

HELP WITH LISTENING: NOTE COMPLETION TASKS

In the listening test, if you have to do a note-taking task, REMEMBER:

- always read the instructions carefully. Think about the speakers and the context.
- to read the questions carefully.
- some of the information you need to understand the text is already written on the page.
- you only need to write between one and three full words for each answer.

1 Before you listen, look at the questions in Part One. What type of information will you need to answer these questions?

- Look at the instructions.
- Are you required to write full sentences?
- How many words will you write in each space?
- How many speakers will you hear? What do you know about them?

Listen to Part One and complete the task.

Part One

You will hear part of a radio interview with a doctor about a form of eye disease called glaucoma. For questions **1–3**, complete the notes with a word or short phrase.

Percentage of people affected: _____ **1**

Why disease is difficult to detect: _____ **2**

When it is usually detected: _____ **3**

---

2 Look at Part Two of the task.

- How is the task different from that in Part One?
- Are the instructions different?
- What type of information will you be listening for to answer these questions?
- How do you think the speaker will present the information?

Listen to Part Two and complete the task.

Part Two

You will hear part of a radio interview with a doctor about a form of eye disease called glaucoma. For questions **4–9**, complete the notes with a word or short phrase.

Three Tests to Check for the Disease

TEST ONE
- makes use of ☐ **4**
- shows any damage to the optic nerve

TEST TWO
- tests the ☐ **5** pressure of the eye
- makes use of ☐ **6**
- measures the resistance

TEST THREE
- checks your ☐ **7**
- makes use of ☐ **8**
- checks for ☐ **9**

3 Look at Part Three of the task. What type of information does each of the questions require? Check the instructions.

📼 Listen to Part Three and complete the task.

Part Three

You will hear part of a radio interview with a doctor about a form of eye disease called glaucoma. For questions **10–17**, complete the notes with a word or short phrase.

How long the disease has been known ☐ **10**

Old way of testing: only ☐ **11** tested.

Groups particularly at risk of disease:
- people with a ☐ **12**
- people with diabetes
- ☐ **13** people
- older people
- people with ☐ **14**

Qualities of a 'user-friendly' ☐ **15** test:
- simple
- cheap
- ☐ **16**

EXAMPRACTICE 1 ▰▰▰▰▰▰▰▰▰▰▰▰▰▰▰▰▰▰▰▰▰▰▰▰▰▰▰▰▰▰

▰ 1 In this section you must choose the word or phrase, **A**, **B**, **C** or **D** which best completes each sentence.

1   People began to realize that the cheap way out might turn _____ to be nothing of the sort.

   A up   **B** down   **C** round   **D** out

2   All the evidence _____ the claim that smoking is the biggest preventable cause of death.

   A enrages   **B** outweighs   **C** indicates   **D** supports

3   Smokers are being encouraged to cut down on their _____ of cigarettes.

   A uptake   **B** onset   **C** intake   **D** outset

4   Fear of the dentist is fifth among commonly _____ fears.

   A held   **B** said   **C** kept   **D** told

5   Many dental phobics are unable to _____ the idea of dental work.

   A imagine   **B** realize   **C** enjoy   **D** entertain

6   People continue to think dentists cause pain _____ media coverage to the contrary.

   A although   **B** despite   **C** however   **D** whereas

7   Because of the nature of the pain, nobody seemed to able to put their _____ on the cause.

   A finger   **B** mark   **C** word   **D** name

8   The main aim of the campaign is to raise _____ of the issues involved.

   A knowledge   **B** awareness   **C** attention   **D** acquaintance

9   Screening tests are administered on a regular _____ .

   A way   **B** routine   **C** matter   **D** basis

10   He is having a wisdom tooth removed _____ anaesthetic.

   A by   **B** under   **C** during   **D** through

2 Fill each of the numbered blanks in the passage with **one** suitable word.

Deep-fried Mars Bar

I did not, at first, believe in the deep-fried *Mars Bar*, considering it to be an urban myth, or something made (**1**) _____ by journalists. Then I visited Scotland and saw it with my (**2**) _____ eyes. Indeed, as if that weren't (**3**) _____, I tasted it.

Available at fish and chip shops, it is probably the most cardiologically lethal concoction (**4**) _____ devised, even in a nation as hooked (**5**) _____ its cholesterol as Scotland. 'It doesn't (**6**) _____ if it's healthy or not, if you enjoy it,' explained Lynne Dodd, echoing the general stoicism (**7**) _____ she cheerfully fried a *Mars Bar* for me at Gino's Fish Bar, in Queen Street, Dunoon near Glasgow.

Snickers may also (**8**) _____ deep fried she confided, (**9**) _____ not *Kit Kats* which have a tendency (**10**) _____ explode into the fat, imparting (**11**) _____ chocolate flavour to subsequent batches of chips.

At Gino's, which has (**12**) _____ times dispensed as many as fifty fried *Mars Bars* in a day, the recipe (**13**) _____ a ghastly simplicity.

Heat the fat to more than four hundred degrees. Smother the *Mars Bar* (**14**) _____ a batter of yellow flour, water and seasonings, of the (**15**) _____ used for frying fish. Immerse in the boiling fat for three to four minutes. Serve with chips.

I confess that I (**16**) _____ a very small taste of the confection palatable, with a flavour reminiscent (**17**) _____ a profiterole. A little does, however, (**18**) _____ a long way. Indeed, I think that (**19**) _____ such bar would be quite sufficient to (**20**) _____ the curiosity of a large number of investigators.

3 Fill each of the blanks with a suitable word or phrase.

1 Catherine said that there was no _____ as a safe level of smoking.

2 People with a family history of the condition are more at _____ getting it.

3 In a screening test, people are tested as a matter _____, not because they have a problem.

4 Sorry, I can't make that cake because I've _____ of sugar.

5 It is feared that a low price encourages young people _____ up smoking.

■4 Finish each of the following sentences in such a way that it is as similar as possible in meaning to the sentence printed before it.

Example: Immediately after his departure, things improved.

Answer: No sooner *had he departed than things improved.*

1   Daphne is going to see the dentist who will remove her bad tooth.

Daphne is going to have _____

2   Clare Lodge has not been to the dentist for 18 years.

It is 18 years _____

3   Dr Rich can only treat patients whose headaches are caused by dental problems.

Only _____

4   Until 1950, burgers were not really eaten in Britain.

Only since _____

5   The arrival of the hamburger in America dates from the 1880s.

By the 1880s _____

6   The doctor said Yvonne needed to have three tests.

The doctor said it _____

7   Ron agreed to do the work on condition that he was paid at once.

Ron said, 'As _____'

8   I will give Ben the message immediately he comes back from lunch.

As _____

9   Over the years, untreated dental conditions will deteriorate.

If _____

10   It's imperative that Robin is careful not to eat any meat products.

Robin _____

Call of the Wild

SPEAKING 1

Talking about photographs

1 Look at the pictures and
compare and contrast the
relationship between people
and animals shown in each
one.

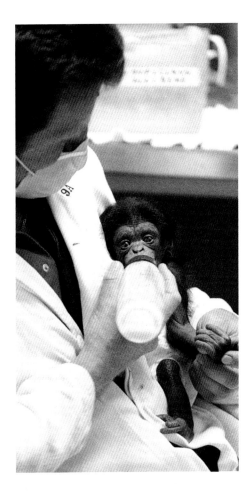

2 To what extent do humans exploit animals? Is this right? avoidable? inevitable?

Talk about:

pets	working animals	circuses	films/TV/advertising
zoos	hunting	factory farming	testing chemicals on animals

3 Which animals make the best pets? Why?

4 Draw up a list of criteria, with about six points in each, for:
  a The ideal pet is one which...
  b The ideal pet owner is someone who...

READING 1
Part One
Reading for gist

Look at this headline. What do you think the article is going to be about?

ONE OF MY PET HATES

When I heard the terrible story of the family attacked by a nine-foot python in a hotel room in San Diego, California, my initial reaction was to blame the hotel management – who increasingly cut costs by hurrying chambermaids through their duties. But even allowing for such carelessness, it would take a very casual cleaner to overlook a two-stone[metric] serpent; for constricting snakes will not blend in with shower curtains, bidets, pile carpet and trouser-presses.

So, I was relieved to discover that the unfortunate victims of the reptile had actually brought it with them; Brad Carter and his pregnant wife, Mary-Ann, and their toddlers, Joshua and Ashley, were sharing one room with their pet python, Selena. Early in the morning, the usually docile serpent, obviously tired of its usual diet of live guinea pigs, plunged its fangs into the ample backside of the sleeping mother. One can only speculate what species of animal it thought it was eating, and how it thought it was going to swallow its prey.

Unsurprisingly, the bite woke Mary-Ann, who describes how she was simultaneously 'frozen with horror' and 'screaming hysterically'. So, the python decided it had better constrict her quickly. Brad then woke up, sized up the situation pretty quickly ('my wife is being eaten by a snake') and started belabouring Selena with a penknife. Eventually, a passing paramedic, Ron Hawkins, decapitated the reptile with a Swiss army knife, that had been bought for his birthday only a fortnight earlier – a happy accident indeed.

Apparently, Brad had purchased Selena from a 'street trader' for $100. She was a happy snake, who liked to lick his face after her guinea pig. 'Like a slippery puppy dog', he said ruefully. But today he is a wiser man, for he knows that it is very rare for a chap to go on holiday, and find his wife being throttled to death by the family puppy dog.

Obvious you might think. But don't be too smug; Brad has his counterparts in Britain,

1 Read the article quickly and underline the names in the box as they occur in the text. What are the relationships between these people and animals?

> Brad Carter   Mary-Ann   Selena
> Joshua   Ashley   Ron Hawkins
> Ann Webb

2 The article can be divided into two main sections. Look back and decide where the division between these two sections comes. What is the main focus of each of the sections?

and plenty of them. Every year, more and more exotic pets are sold. One company, Pet City, has made a fortune selling (among other
50 things) giant boas and pythons (500 last year) chipmunks (350), scorpions (300), and, of course, tarantulas (600).

And, like the many other exotic species you can buy, all these pets are 'harmless', 'friendly' even. Take this statement, for example: 'Tarantulas are not particularly aggressive,' says the honorary secretary of the Tarantula Society, Ann Webb (yes, that is her name). Of course they aren't Ann; they don't
60 have to be. They only need to turn up on your pillow and the instant heart attack will do the rest. There is only one point to owning such an animal, and that is to scare the life out of family and friends.

Yet Pet City will do a 'Tarantula Starter Kit' complete with baby spider, warming pad (for those freezing winters) and 'tunnelling material' for just £3300. Let's face it. The rest of us will just have to live in fear, simply so
70 that the Brad Carters of this world will be able to boast about the exotic pets they keep in their houses, and take away on holiday, with them.

Part Two
Comprehension

1 Now read more carefully and decide if each of the statements 1–8 match the writer's opinion or not.

1 The problem with the snake was the fault of the hotel management.
2 The hotel staff should have noticed the snake.
3 The snake probably attacked Mrs Carter because it was hungry.
4 Brad Carter was totally incapable of dealing with the situation.
5 Brad now realizes that buying the snake was a mistake.
6 The *Pet City* company has been successful at selling exotic pets.
7 The information given by the Tarantula Society is inaccurate.
8 People are buying exotic pets for the wrong reasons.

2 Answer these questions.
1 Why does the writer use the pronoun 'one' in line 21?
2 What is the writer referring to when he uses the words 'its prey' in line 23?
3 What is the meaning of the phrasal verb 'sized up'? (line 29)
4 What is the 'happy accident' referred to in lines 35–36?
5 Who is 'you' in line 45?
6 What does 'these' in line 54 refer to?
7 Why does the writer add the phrase in brackets in line 58?

3 The writer uses different words and expressions each time he talks about Brad Carter's pet. Look back at the article and underline each of these. Why does the writer use all these different forms?

4 What is the writer's attitude to the following?
a hotels   c Selena   e Ann Webb
b Brad Carter d *Pet City*

Find examples in the text which show this. Do you agree with him?

WRITING 1
Summary

1   What do you think about the style of writing used in the piece? How does the writer use this to get his point across? Think about:

- the intended audience;
- the effect the writer wants to have on that audience;
- the use of irony.

2   Look at the words and phrases in inverted commas in the article and for each one decide why these have been used.

3   What is the main point that the writer is trying to make in this article? In a paragraph of 60-90 words, explain the writer's attitude to the trade in exotic pets, giving his reasons. Use your own words.

GRAMMAR 1
Relative pronouns

■1   Look at these sentences from the article. What does *who* refer to in each of them?

   a   My initial reaction was to blame the hotel management who increasingly cut costs.
   b   Selena was a happy snake who liked to lick his face.
   c   The bite woke Mary-Ann who describes how she was frozen with terror.

■2   What other relative pronouns are there? When do we use *who* and when do we use these other words?

■3   Join each of these sentences using an appropriate relative pronoun.

   1   Ron Hawkins used the penknife. It had been bought for his birthday.
   2   Ann Webb was talking about tarantulas. She says they are not particularly aggressive.
   3   Selena is the snake's name. It bit Mary-Ann.
   4   Joshua is a toddler. His father owned the snake.
   5   *Pet City* is a shop. It sells tarantula starter kits.
   6   Selena was a snake. She was used to eating guinea pigs.
   7   The story takes place in a hotel. It is in San Diego, California.

■4   Complete each sentence with a suitable relative pronoun.

   1   The hotel _____ the story takes place is in California.
   2   It was the Carter family _____ brought the snake into the hotel.
   3   It was Mary-Ann _____ first raised the alarm.
   4   It was Ron _____ knife was used to kill Selena.
   5   It is *Pet City* _____ sells 500 tarantulas per year.
   6   It is tarantulas _____ sell in the largest numbers.
   7   It is the Tarantula Society _____ secretary is called Ann Webb.
   8   It was Selena _____ was feeling hungry
   9   But, it's in Britain _____ *Pet City* have been selling lots of exotic pets.

   📖 N.B. The Workbook has further work on relative pronouns

SPEAKING 2
Expressing opinions

1   Look at this advertisement which was placed in a national newspaper. Who do you think placed the advertisement?

A PUPPY IS FOR LIFE NOT JUST FOR YOUR BIRTHDAY

2   What message is it giving?

3   Is the message relevant to exotic pets?

4   What problems do people face when they buy unsuitable pets? What are the solutions to these problems?

LISTENING 1
Multiple choice

1   You will hear a radio interview with a woman who has made a film about the problems associated with the keeping of baby orang-utans as pets. For questions **1–7**, choose the alternative **A**, **B**, **C** or **D** which you think fits best according to what you hear.

1   What was Sarah's original aim in making the film?

   A to inform people about orang-utans.
   B to investigate one particular relationship.
   C to help the foundation raise money.
   D to expose the illegal trade in animals.

2   How did Sarah feel when she first met Dai Dai?

   A disgusted
   B amazed
   C frightened
   D delighted

3   What impressed Sarah most about Dai Dai?

   A the clothes she wore
   B how much she understood
   C how obedient she was
   D her musical talent

4   Why did Mrs Chang decide not to keep Dai Dai?

   A She was concerned about the future.
   B She was in financial difficulties.
   C She didn't have the necessary commitment.
   D She was losing control of the animal.

5   What is the main aim of the centre Dai Dai went to in Borneo?

   A To protect the animals from tourists.
   B To make sure the animals are healthy.
   C To make the animals less dependent on humans.
   D To show the animals what to eat in the wild.

6   What does the episode at the end of the film show?

   A How close Mrs Chang and Dai Dai were.
   B How Dai Dai wasn't ready for release.
   C How little Mrs Chang understood Dai Dai.
   D How like humans orang-utans are.

7   How can we best summarize Sarah's attitude towards Mrs Chang?

   A Mrs Chang's behaviour was appalling.
   B Mrs Chang's concern was touching.
   C Mrs Chang's opinions were unimportant.
   D Mrs Chang's feelings were unnatural.

2   How does the story of Dai Dai and Mrs Chang make you feel?

Talk about:
- How can situations like this be avoided?
- Do you know of any similar stories?
- What problems do you think Dai Dai will face in the wild?
- What will Mrs Chang's life be like now?

Cause and result

1 Read the introduction to the radio interview. Complete the text with a word from the box; some words can be used more than once. Then listen to check.

with	there	which	where	this	such	that

Some years ago, (**1**) _____ was a popular childen's TV soap opera in the Far East (**2**) _____ starred a pet orang-utan. (**3**) _____ led to a demand for (**4**) _____ animals (**5**) _____ resulted in enormous smuggling from the island of Borneo to other Pacific rim countries (**6**) _____ the babies were bought as luxury pets. (**7**) _____ fashion has now resulted in a large number of orang-utans (**8**) _____ are proving too much for their owners to cope (**9**) _____ .

2 Now answer these questions.

1 When do we use *which*, and when do we use *this*?

2 When should *that* be used instead of *this*?

3 Why did the speaker use *such* and not *these*?

4 What is the difference between *led to* and *resulted in*? Why did the speaker use both these forms?

3 Read these sentences about tarantulas. Link each sentence using suitable pronouns and the forms *resulted in* and *led to* to make a paragraph.

An episode of the Australian soap opera *Neighbours*, which is popular in Britain, showed two girls buying a pet tarantula.

Demand for tarantulas in Britain increased.

Tarantula sales at the *Pet City* shop quadrupled.

Most of the spiders were bought by teenage girls and young mothers.

Many people have been bitten by tarantulas.

The bite is painful like a bee sting.

Many tarantulas have been killed or abandoned by owners who no longer want them.

📖 N.B. The Workbook has further work on expressing cause and result.

HELP WITH CLOZE PASSAGES

1 Each of the exercises in this section is designed to develop skills that will help you to do the cloze tests in the examination.

You will be looking at a number of short texts connected with the growing and production of tea.

First discuss the topic of tea with your partner. Talk about:

- where tea is grown
- the plant itself
- different types of tea
- where tea is popular
- how to make a cup of tea

2 Now look at this paragraph about the history of tea drinking.

1 Read the paragraph through first to understand the whole context, but ignore the missing words.

2 Now think about the missing words. For each space, decide if the missing word is:

- a noun
- a verb
- an adjective
- a preposition
- another type of word

Don't write the word yet, just identify the <u>type</u> of word that is missing.

The Legend of Tea Drinking

The legends surrounding the origins of tea drinking are almost as
(**1**) _____ as the different types, or blends, of tea available today,
and they (**2**) _____ from region to region. Indian and Japanese tales
(**3**) _____ a devout Buddhist priest called Bodhidharma,
(**4**) _____ was attempting a seven-year, sleepless contemplation of
Buddha when he began to (**5**) _____ drowsy. In the Indian version, he
plucked a (**6**) _____ leaves from the tree under which he sat and,
(**7**) _____ chewing them, found that the sleepiness (**8**)_____
him. The Japanese story is slightly different; the priest cutting (**9**) _____
his drooping eyelids in frustration and throwing them (**10**) _____ the
ground. Where his eyelids landed, two tea bushes sprang (**11**) _____,
and their leaves had the property (**12**) _____ fending off sleep.

3 Look at the words in the box. Divide them into nouns, verbs, prepositions adjectives and other words.

describe	feel	few	to	left	on
of	off	plentiful	up	vary	who

4 Put one of the words from the box into each of the blanks in the text.

■3 In this continuation of the text, all the prepositions have been omitted.

1 First read the paragraph to get an idea of the context.

2 Now draw a line to show the places where you think there should be prepositions, but don't worry about which prepositions to use. The first one has been done for you as an example.

The Chinese legend, however, is the most popular and certainly the most believable. /The year 2737 BC, the Emperor Shen Nung was boiling some water the tree called Camellia Sinensis when some leaves fell the pot. He found that the result was a pleasant new beverage which was a great improvement boiled water. Modern tea comes the same species which the emperor discovered. The Chinese discovered that it could produce a wide range flavours and characteristics. This is achieved growing the plants different soils and climates and different altitudes rather like vines. Indeed many tea varieties are often compared fine wines.

3 Look at the prepositions in the box. Which will fit into each of the blanks you have indicated?

at	in	into	from	under	to	on	through	of

■4 In the next piece of text, ten words are in the wrong form. e.g. a verb form instead of a noun, or an adverb instead of an adjective, etc.

1 First read the paragraph to get an idea of the context.

2 Then read the paragraph again carefully and underline the words which seem to be wrong.

3 Finally write in the correct forms of the words. The first one has been done for you as an example.

In time, the Chinese <u>perfection</u> three quite distinct types of tea by variation the processing technique; these were green tea which is unfermented, red tea which is partially fermented and black tea which is full fermented. Black tea, which was tradition produced solely in China, spread to India in 1839 and is now cultivated and processes all over the world. Tea can be growth in almost any region with a warm tropical or sub-tropical climate and plenty of rainfall. Left uncultivated, the tea plant – which is reality a tree – would reach a high of around nine metres. It is kept well pruned, however, to make it easy to pick. After about three to five years, depends on the altitude, the plant is ready for pick, when the top bud of the bush and the adjacent two leaves are plucked off.

perfected
_____
_____
_____
_____
_____
_____
_____
_____
_____

5 In the next text, choose the best alternative **A**, **B**, or **C** to complete each of the numbered blanks.

People often ask how to (**1**) _____ about making the perfect cup of tea. Making a good cup of tea is not difficult, (**2**) _____ there are a number of golden rules which (**3**) _____ is as well to follow. Firstly, only use fresh, high-quality tea which should be kept in an airtight container, (**4**) _____ from any strong smelling items. Always use fresh cold water (**5**) _____ hot or reheated water contains less oxygen and gives a flat, stale taste. Warm your teapot (**6**) _____ rinsing it in hot water. This ensures the water stays (**7**) _____ boiling point when it touches the tea. It is important to use the right amount of tea. You should put one teaspoonful of tea (**8**) _____ person into the pot, (**9**) _____ an extra spoonful 'for the pot', as it is called. Finally, do (**10**) _____ sure your teapot is clean, but never put it in a dishwasher or use detergents on it, rinsing it in cold water is usually sufficient.

1	**A** start	**B** go	**C** get
2	**A** also	**B** or	**C** but
3	**A** it	**B** there	**C** people
4	**A** away	**B** afar	**C** alone
5	**A** not	**B** as	**C** while
6	**A** or	**B** by	**C** and
7	**A** on	**B** to	**C** at
8	**A** per	**B** for	**C** each
9	**A** added	**B** adding	**C** addition
10	**A** makes	**B** making	**C** make

6 Now fill each of the numbered blanks in this last paragraph with **one** suitable word as you would in the examination.

Remember:
- read through the passage first to get an idea of the context;
- think about the form of the words which are missing;
- check that the word you choose fits into the grammar of the sentence;
- check that the word you choose fits into the sense of the passage.

Don't forget that when making a pot of tea, brewing time is critical. Pour in the boiling water and (**1**) _____ the tea brew for three to five minutes, (**2**) _____ on the size of the tea-leaf being used. If the strength is not to (**3**) _____ liking, adjust the amount of tea used, (**4**) _____ than the brewing time.

Another thing which is important (**5**) _____ to stir the tea before (**6**) _____ it out. Some people turn the pot three times one way and three times the other, which (**7**) _____ the same job. Tea will taste unpleasantly stewed (**8**) _____ left in the pot for more than ten minutes. It is also better (**9**) _____ to use a tea cosy or other form of teapot cover, as this will simply speed (**10**) _____ the stewing process.

Now look back at your answers. Which of them has made:
- a verb and preposition which always go together (a collocation)?
- a grammatical phrase used in comparisons?
- an idiomatic phrase?
- a phrasal verb?

Multiple choice

1 Look at this book cover. Talk about the type of book it could be, the sort of people who might buy it and people's reaction to it.

2 If you were a journalist interviewing the author of this book, what questions would you want to ask? Make a list.

3 You are going to read an article based on such an interview. What do you expect the style or tone of the article to be? Read quickly to check.

Knitting with Dog Hair

Better a sweater from a **dog** *you know and love than a* **sheep** *you'll never meet*

STOP VACUUMING & START KNITTING

Shaggy Dog Story

Summer is a sleepy time for the publishing world, but one book, only recently released, has already gone into a second impression. In fact, 'Knitting with Dog Hair' has become a surprise cult hit. From the title, it sounds like another work of gritty Glasgow realism from the school of Irvine Walsh – until one sees the cover which has a dachshund wearing a tam o'shanter. Then the appalling
10 **truth dawns. This book is serious.**

Indeed, one of the writers of this small but information-packed volume is Kendall Crolius, a senior vice-president of a major American advertising company. Inside is a complete guide to each stage in creating clothing from 'a dog you know and love rather than a sheep you'll never meet' as the book puts it – from picking up the hairball under the sofa to spinning the yarn. At the back of the book are patterns for scarves, mittens and jumpers, with the finished results proudly
20 modelled by the dog owners. There's even an exhaustive guide to which dogs provide the best yarn. Readers learn that the Rottweiler, 'calm and intelligent by nature, has a very short, fine undercoat that can be spun when mixed with longer fibres, but do make sure you have his full co-operation before you pick up the brush'.

I felt I already knew Kendall, and indeed, her family, from the smudgy black-and-white photographs which are littered throughout the book. There's little Martha, her daughter, with mittens from a Samoyed puppy,
30 Trevor, her eight-year-old son, in a jumper knitted from two-ply great pyrenees, and one must not forget Cynthia,

Kendall's sister who models a 'tam' made from Ollie. But when it was mentioned that Kendall was in London on a high-powered mission for her company, I couldn't pass up the opportunity of meeting her.

If the publicity pictures of Kendall Crolius, and co-author Anne
40 Montgomery, look apple-pie normal, rather than dog-crazed rustics, I still wasn't expecting the perfectly manicured vision of corporate America that greeted me at the front door. Kendall was dressed in an elegant cream suit – exactly the sort of attire one could not wear anywhere near a dog. Perhaps the whole project was merely a warped marketing ploy
50 to sell more knitting needles.

This whole notion, however, was instantly knocked on the head. Kendall was only too happy to tell me the benefits of knitting with dog hair. This isn't just knitting. It's a cause.

The whole 'dog-hair thing' as Kendall calls it, began 15 years ago, when she learnt how to spin. Kendall says this in an off-hand way, but the only excuse for an advertising executive to resort to spinning is watching Sleeping Beauty too many times. 'Spinning was becoming increasingly popular,' Kendall explained 'and I do like to master new skills'. But why spinning, when one can buy wool from a shop? 'Oh, it's not that I thought I'd need to make my family clothes, it's just that it's so fundamental. You can't go through a day without dealing with fibres. And it's very therapeutic. It forces you to wind down, and the great thing about spinning is you can take it out onto the porch and the kids will come out and we'll tell stories'. A craft for our times? 'Exactly.'

It was on a spinning course, in Brooklyn, that Kendall first heard about the amazing properties of dog fur. 'Our teacher happened to mention that one could spin dog hair. Everyone went 'hah, hah', but I thought 'hmmmm'. There aren't a lot of sheep in New York and buying yarn can get expensive and we already had a golden retriever... in fact this is golden retriever,' said Kendall, brandishing a coppery-brown scarf. Although the dog departed life some years ago, she lingers on in Kendall's wardrobe.

'I smile every time I wear the scarf. There are people who stuff their dogs - I don't think I could do that - but this is like carrying a lock of hair. It's a lot of hair, sure, but it is that little touchstone that makes you feel connected and it looks quite beautiful when worn with my camel-hair coat. It's been quite a conversation piece.'

Kendall now has a chocolate-brown labrador, Cadbury. Although she stresses that she really didn't want a dog 'just to make sweaters', she does accept that it was fortunate when Cadbury turned out to have long hair of the sort that covered upholstery in a fine layer. The hair, by the way, is gathered after it has been shed, or as a result of grooming with a brush. I was under the false and truly horrible misapprehension that they sheared the dogs like sheep.

The book, which was 'written on a lap top on business trips back and forth to Michigan' has been an immediate success in the States, after being turned down by countless publishers. One has to face facts. There are many people knitting up their dogs. Suddenly I felt the surreal quality of this conversation was overwhelming. Surely it was all a joke? Kendall was unrelenting. 'We did want this to be a fun read. But we're not kidding. Look upon it as recycling. This is just a how-to-manual.'

4 Now read the article again more carefully and answer the questions **1–6**. Choose the answer, **A**, **B**, **C** or **D** which you think fits best.

1 The journalist believes that the book has become successful because

   A it was released at a quiet time.
   B it has an appealing title.
   C it is a fashionable book to buy.
   D it has an intriguing cover.

2 The main aim of the book is to

   A prove what can be achieved.
   B give instructions on a number of processes.
   C give advice on the choice of materials.
   D provide examples of successful projects.

3 How did the journalist feel on meeting Kendall Crolius?

   A surprised at how she was dressed
   B comforted by her normal appearance
   C pleased that she resembled her photos
   D relieved that she had no dog with her

4 Why did Kendall first take up spinning?

   A She wanted to be able to make something useful.
   B It was something the whole family could learn.
   C She was looking for a relaxing hobby.
   D It was a skill that few people could master.

5 What was Kendall's main motive for taking up the spinning of dog's hair?

   A She thought it would save money.
   B She was sentimental about dogs.
   C She wanted to impress her friends.
   D She could see the business potential.

6 What does the journalist remain unconvinced about?

   A how the dog hair is collected
   B how Kendall chose her current dog
   C how seriously to take the book
   D how popular the book really is

5 In your own words, explain what the writer means by each of these expressions as used in the article (paragraph numbers in brackets):

    a the appalling truth dawns (1)
    b littered through the book (3)
    c a high-powered mission (3)
    d apple-pie normal (4)
    e dog-crazed rustics (4)
    f vision of corporate America (4)
    g a marketing ploy (4)
    h that little touchstone (8)
    i truly horrible misapprehension (9)
    j the surreal quality (10)

1 How would you feel about wearing a pullover made from dog's hair?

2 Should we wear leather, fur, wool and other animal-based fabrics when synthetic alternatives are available? Talk to you partner saying what you think and why.

PHRASAL VERBS 1
With 'up' and 'down'

1 The article you have read contains four phrasal verbs which include the prepositions *up* or *down*. Look back and find them. Match the meaning of each phrasal verb to a verb in the box.

a arrive	**d** depress	**f** miss	**i** relax
b collapse	**e** gather	**g** reduce	**j** assess
c demolish		**h** refuse	

2 Complete each sentence with either *up* or *down*. Then match the meaning of the phrasal verbs you have formed with a verb from the box above.

1 At the end of the interview, Melanie broke _____ in tears.

2 The company decided to cut _____ on the amount of money spent on advertising.

3 Although I waited for half an hour, Harry failed to show _____ .

4 The old houses were being pulled _____ to make way for the new stadium.

5 Her friends' nasty comments about her new boyfriend were beginning to get Mary _____ .

6 Before taking any action, they decided to size _____ the situation.

    N.B. The Workbook has further examples of phrasal verbs with *up* and *down*.

USE OF ENGLISH 1
Cloze passage

1 Look at the photographs. Discuss what you think is happening in each one and what you think the outcome will be.

2 Match these headlines to the photographs.

Fishermen to the rescue of feathered friend in need   *Mass strandings spark frantic rescue missions*

3 Look at the words in the box. Put them into four categories depending on whether they are **a** nouns/pronouns, **b** verbs, **c** prepositions or **d** other words.

at	back	becomes	brought	carrying	had	in	long	no	~~over~~	one
or	rate	result	ringing	their		to	up	when	which	with

4 Look at the text. Before you try to put in the missing words decide which gaps need prepositions. Then look back at the list in the box and decide which preposition will fit each gap. The first one has been done for you as an example.

Repeat the process for the other three categories.

Strandings

All (**0**) *over* the world, strandings of dolphins and whales are becoming more common and environmentalists claim that this may be Nature (**1**) _____ the alarm bells, believing it is the sea itself (**2**) _____ is enduring a slow death (**3**) _____ about by pollution. Dolphins dying off America and in the Mediterranean were nearly all infected (**4**) _____ a virus, but they were also (**5**) _____ a heavy pollution burden which (**6**) _____ suppressed their immune systems.

Individual strandings are mainly the (**7**) _____ of illness or injury. The animals cannot either navigate (**8**) _____ swim properly and accidentally come ashore. It is even possible that they may choose to strand themselves as a response (**9**) _____ their condition. In the southern hemisphere, mass strandings of these animals are common and everywhere (**10**) _____ plight sparks frantic rescue missions to refloat them by well-meaning humans. Such strandings happen (**11**) _____ the animals are in a large group and their leader (**12**) _____ disoriented and swims ashore. They then all follow and, as (**13**) _____ as the leader remains stranded, (**14**) _____ amount of work by human rescuers will persuade the others to go (**15**) _____ to sea.

(**16**) _____ piece of good news is that when people succeed (**17**) _____ refloating stranded whales, the survival (**18**) _____ can be encouraging. In New Zealand, where most stranded whales are fit and merely lost, (**19**) _____ to ninety per cent survive. One signal, at least, that all may not be wrong (**20**) _____ sea.

🔊 HELP WITH LISTENING: SENTENCE COMPLETION TASKS

■ 1 Look back at Unit One. Compare the rubric and questions for this listening task with those on page 16. What is the same? What is different?

You will hear part of a radio programme about attempts to save stranded whales in Britain. For each of the questions **1–11**, complete the sentences with a word or short phrase.

The Whale and dolphin protection society aims to create a network

of what it calls [_____ **1**] across the country.

Volunteers are trained using a full-length inflatable whale which is

[_____ **2**] to make it heavy.

Rescuers put a [_____ **3**] under the whale so that it can be

moved out to sea.

To ensure their survival, stranded whales should not be allowed to

[_____ **4**] .

Without help, stranded whales always die because, even at sea, they are unable to move

[_____ **5**] .

Teresa says that during the rescue, whales don't appear to be [_____ **6**] .

The rescuers usually release the whale in water which

is approximately [_____ **7**] .

More than two thousand whales in New Zealand have been saved by

what is called the [_____ **8**] .

Most whales which come ashore in Britain are [_____ **9**] .

One problem is that many live strandings occur in [_____ **10**] places.

Teresa is surprised at the [_____ **11**] of volunteers training today.

■ 2 Look at these student answers to question 10. Decide whether each of them is a good answer or not and why.

places which are remote   *no people*   *turn up in remote*
really remote   *remote*   *where there aren't people*

In the listening test, if you have to do a sentence-completion task, REMEMBER:
- always read the instructions carefully. Think about the speakers and the context to help you feel ready.
- read the questions and think about what the answers will be, both in terms of the meaning and what type of word or phrase is needed.
- a lot of the information is included in the question, both before and after the gap. Be careful not to repeat it.
- you only need to write between one and three full words for each answer.
- check that the sentence you have created is grammatically correct and that the words you have written are spelt correctly.

VOCABULARY 1
Idiomatic phrases

1 Do you know the name of this bird? Why is it famous?

2 Look at this sentence.

I'm afraid the project has no future; it's as dead as a dodo.

3 Now complete each idiomatic phrase with a word from the box.

bee	bull	cat	chicken	dog
fish	fly	lamb	pig	snake

1 It's time to be brave and take the _____ by the horns.

2 Terry went meekly into the exam room, like a _____ to the slaughter.

3 Misfortune was to _____ Charles for the rest of his life.

4 From this point the road begins to _____ down hill to the coast.

5 I've eaten too much, I've made a real _____ of myself.

6 Philip's such a gentle man, he wouldn't hurt a _____ .

7 Grandfather looked like a _____ out of water at the disco.

8 John's got the big match tomorrow, but I'm sure he's going to _____ out at the last minute and stay at home.

9 Carol arrived at the party and made a _____ line for the sandwiches as she hadn't eaten for hours.

10 Lisa walked in tentatively, like a _____ on a hot tin roof.

   📖 N.B. The Workbook has further work on animal vocabulary.

SPEAKING 3
Discussing pros and cons

1 What can be done to help animals that are in danger of extinction?

Which of these ideas would you favour? What are the advantages and drawbacks of each idea?

- ban hunting
- create nature reserves
- go back to natural farming methods
- stop the expansion of cultivation
- breed animals in zoos
- set up captive breeding programmes and then release animals into the wild

2 Talk to your partner about:

- What good can animal welfare organizations do?
- How can people help them? Financially? Practically?
- What different types of organization are there?
- Why do some people not support them?
- Would you be willing to help an animal welfare organization?

WRITING 2
Formal letters

1 Look at these quotes made by representatives of various animal welfare organizations in a magazine article. Which of the representatives would agree with each of the statements **1–7** below. Some of the statements reflect the views of two organizations.

1 Most of our work involves research. ☐

2 It is not our normal policy to use our funds for saving injured animals. ☐ ☐

3 Our organization's aim is to save animals' lives at all costs. ☐

4 Our organization's main concern is the countryside in general. ☐

5 Some well-intentioned people have the wrong attitude towards animals. ☐

6 We do not believe in keeping animals in cages. ☐ ☐

7 We try to understand how animals feel. ☐

REPRESENTATIVE A
We take in injured, harmed, unwanted, run over, shot, mentally damaged animals of all kinds. If a bird's lost a wing, we don't count it as a reason why it should die. The only difference between this sanctuary and others is, if you bring us a heap of bones which is bird, by the time you've got back into your car, we have decided how we're going to make it into a bird again, and we won't have wrung its neck before you get home.

REPRESENTATIVE B
If somebody finds, say, a rabbit that's been run over and has a broken leg, the last thing one should do is take it to a vet and waste money on trying to pin it together and then put it in a cage. The kindest thing to do is knock it on the head. Now that would horrify the average town dweller, but what we're trying to do is preserve genuine rural habitats. I'm afraid the trouble is, and it may seem unkind to say it in this way, but certain people are merely over-sentimental about animals, and it really tells you more about the people concerned than it does about the well-being of wildlife.

REPRESENTATIVE C
As far as we're concerned the important thing is quality of life. If we feel an animal can be repaired relatively quickly, and returned to the wild, then we'll help it. What we hate is keeping animals in captivity, and if we think that's going to be the case, we'd rather put it to sleep. If an animal hasn't got its freedom, its whole reason for being has completely gone and it's unlikely to be happy or lead a proper life. People are very good at projecting their emotions onto animals and looking at them and deciding whether they're happy or not. An animal may look happy if you throw some food in to its cage, but if that animal's natural instinct is to hunt for it, this will not feel right for the animal. Living in captivity is really stressful for animals. It has to be.

REPRESENTATIVE D
It was only during the oil spill off the coast that we really began to get involved in animal rescue. And we were using about 160 litres of water per bird to get them cleaned up so that they could be released again. We actually did some very rough sums and came up with a figure of about £35 per bird to wash it, and, of course, this whole operation was quite outside our normal sphere of activity. But, as a wildlife organization we couldn't just sit there and watch the birds suffer what would be a lingering death. So we hope that people will help us to pay for clearing up that mess, by lending financial support to our regular study programmes, which suffered as a result.

2 Which of the organizations do you think has the best ideas? Choose the one which appeals to you most.

How much do you know about your chosen organization?

3 If you were thinking of offering financial or practical help to this organization, what else would you like to know about it? Make a list.

4 Write a letter to your chosen organization, explaining:

- who you are
- how you heard about the organization
- why you are interested
- what information you want

5 Before you write, talk about these questions with your partner.

1   Will the letter be formal? semi-formal? informal?

2   How should the letter begin? Choose the best opening from **A**, **B** or **C**.

A

> To whom it may concern:
>
>   I write with reference to the…

B

> Dear Sir/Madam,
>
>   I am writing to express my interest…

C

> Dear animal lovers,
>
>   I read the bit about you in the…

3   How many paragraphs will the letter have?

4   What will be the focus of each paragraph?

5   How will the paragraphs be introduced and linked together?

6   How will the list of questions be presented?

7   How should the letter end? Choose the best close from **A**, **B** or **C**.

A

> Write soon,
>
>   Best wishes

B

> Looking forward to hearing from you,
>
>   Yours faithfully

C

> I remain,
>
>   Very truly yours

📖 N. B. The Workbook has further work on formal and informal expressions.

EXAM PRACTICE 2

1 In this section, you must choose the word or phrase **A**, **B**, **C** or **D** which best completes each sentence.

1 The Society is putting _____ a nationwide network of volunteer groups.

    A together   **B** through   **C** around   **D** about

2 We are seeing in the _____ of fifteen to twenty whale strandings per year.

    A area   **B** region   **C** range   **D** vicinity

3 Once in the water, it only takes a _____ of minutes to release the whale.

    A a question   **B** a trifle   **C** an amount   **D** a matter

4 The book has a number of knitting _____ which those wishing to make garments can follow.

    A models   **B** patterns   **C** designs   **D** templates

5 It would _____ a very casual cleaner to overlook a snake in a hotel bedroom.

    A take   **B** see   **C** make   **D** have

6 There's so much more to the film than the filmmaker _____ out to achieve.

    A took   **B** set   **C** began   **D** got

7 Whales cannot _____ themselves into reverse; they can't go backwards.

    A turn   **B** put   **C** swim   **D** take

8 This is a picture of our dog, Ollie, _____ hair was used to make this pullover.

    A which   **B** whom   **C** whose   **D** where

9 Orang-utans have a good _____ of smell.

    A ability   **B** skill   **C** sense   **D** power

10 Mrs Chang had given up her job _____ look after Dai Dai.

    A due to   **B** according to   **C** owing to   **D** in order to

■ **2** Fill each of the numbered blanks in the passage with **one** suitable word.

Suspect is blue large and hairy

A Peruvian blue-backed tarantula spider which escaped inside an English magistrate's court in November and was thought to (**1**) _____ died from the rigours of an English winter, has made a comeback (**2**) _____ the height of a fraud trial.

A 'large hairy spider' scuttled along a skirting board (**3**) _____ the defendant, a 47-year-old arachnophobe, was listening to evidence. Barney Cosgrave, the solicitor (**4**) _____ client was taken home after the hearing suffering (**5**) _____ shock, said, 'We're all thinking of coming in (**6**) _____ rubber bands or cycle clips on (**7**) _____ trousers next week'.

(**8**) _____ eight-legged intruder was initially thought to be a harmless raft spider, Britain's largest, but not venomous, species, (**9**) _____ events took a more exciting (**10**) _____ whe the magistrate's clerk reported the incident. The connection was then (**11**) _____ with a young man who (**12**) _____ his pet tarantula into the courthouse in a plastic box, last November, quite legitimately, and later reported that both spider and box (**13**) _____ disappeared.

(**14**) _____ of the Natural History Museum's leading spider specialists was consulted and it was learnt that this is (**15**) _____ a placid spider and people would be well-advised not to handle it. (**16**) _____ its venom is mild for most people, it is much (**17**) _____ aggressive than the Mexican red-kneed tarantula, the one some people allow to crawl over their hands.

The court was (**18**) _____ over the weekend with a penetrating chemical, but a search of the building's nooks and crannies yesterday revealed (**19**) _____ corpse. The Clerk was, however, confident that users of the court were not at (**20**) _____ from a venomous nip.

■ **3** Fill each of the blanks with a suitable word or phrase.
1 There's more to Kendall Crolius than meets _____ .
2 As luck would _____ Ron Hawkins was passing with his Swiss knife.
3 You won't get him to change his mind, he's as _____ mule.
4 Jenny's very shrewd, you can't _____ her eyes.
5 This brand of coffee is a great improvement _____ one you bought last week.

4 For each of the sentences below, write a new sentence as similar as possible in meaning to the original sentence, but using the word given. This word **must not be altered** in any way.

Example: A lot of people attended the meeting.

turnout

Answer: There was a very good turnout for the meeting.

1 I reacted negatively to the story at first.
initial

_____

2 Illness and injury lead to most individual whale strandings.
result

_____

3 Was it a successful day from your point of view?
concerned

_____

4 The book contains a complete guide to each stage of the process.
step

_____

5 A high proportion of whale rescues are successful.
rate

_____

5 Finish each of the following sentences in such a way that it is as similar as possible in meaning to the sentence printed before it.

Example: Immediately after his departure things improved.

Answer: No sooner *had he departed than things improved.*

1 Do you think the whale is likely to survive?
What are the whale's _____

2 Sarah was introduced to Mrs Chang by the Foundation.
It was the _____

3 The pontoon system has saved in excess of 2000 animals.
More than _____

4 The whale showed no sign of being in any discomfort.
There _____

5 Brad Carter bought the snake from this man.
This is the man who _____

A Word in your Ear

SPEAKING 1

Expressing opinions

Talk to your partner about:

- the advantages of knowing a foreign language
- the problems people have in learning a foreign language
- good and bad ways of learning a foreign language

READING 1

Matching

1 You are going to read an article about language called 'Wordtraps'. Look at the pictures. Each one is related to the article in some way. Talk to your partner about:

- what you can see;
- what the picture makes you think of;
- how each picture might be connected with the topic of language.

Wordtraps

Human beings can say what they want when they want, at least in theory. All normal humans can produce and understand any number of new words and sentences, and use language without having to stop and think about it. But, in reality, humans may be subconsciously trapped by the particular language they speak. The question is, do different languages merely use different words and grammar systems to talk about the same things, or do the differences between languages actually reflect different ways of seeing the world?

The American linguist, Whorf, put forward the latter as a theory using the example of the American-Indian language, Hopi. An English phrase such as, 'They stayed 10 days' translated into Hopi becomes, 'They stayed until the eleventh day' or 'They left after the tenth day'. But actually this only proves that Hopi language expresses 'time' in a different way to English; that the Hopi language has made use of a different system for expressing what is essentially the same idea. Whorf didn't find a way of testing whether Hopi Indians actually perceived the idea of time itself in a different way.

Of course, it's very difficult to imagine other ways of perceiving time, which is a symptom of something else which is generally true of language. Humans behave like the 'Frog in the Well' in the Chinese folk tale. The frog lived all its life in the well until one day it hopped out and was astonished to find what a limited view of the world it had always had.

Humans create their own limited mental pictures of the world which are reflected in language. The word 'week' is often quoted as an example of this. A week has no concrete reality in the outside world. Yet most native speakers of English have a mental model of a sequence of seven days,

2 Read the article quickly then find and underline the references to the pictures on page 41.

3 Now read the article again. Look at the list of points **A – G**. What point is illustrated by each of the references **1–7**?

1 Hopi Indians   _C_

2 Frog in the Well   ___

3 Incas   ___

4 Liquid in a Container   ___

5 Octopus   ___

6 Game of Chess   ___

7 Spider's Web   ___

A That the use of certain expressions reflects the mental image people have of their feelings.

B Some cultures may define familiar ideas in different ways.

C That some languages may express the same idea in different ways.

D That in using language, we use a small part of a larger system.

E That the use of certain words may actually give us a wrong idea about something.

F That our understanding of language depends on our experience of the world.

G That certain words are used because we all recognize a familiar image.

which is divided into two chunks, five working days followed by two rest days, the 'weekend' – or sometimes six working days followed by one rest day. They have this idealized notion of a week, even though they may organize their own working life quite differently. In contrast, an Inca week had 10 days, nine working days followed by market day, on which the king changed wives.

It has been suggested that powerful mental images may be created and preserved by metaphors. Consider the emotion of anger. This is often envisaged as heated liquid in a container, as in the phrases, 'Mark's anger simmered', 'Helen seethed with rage' or 'Neil's blood boiled'. Overheated liquid is liable to burst out, as in 'Mary blew her top', 'Matthew exploded'. Such metaphors reflect genuine mental images, according to psycholinguistic experiments. When asked about an idiom such as 'John hit the roof', native English speakers imagine containers bursting open and their contents spouting upwards. They do not imagine a person with springs on his feet hitting his head on the ceiling. But this 'liquid in a container' image of anger is not universal. In some parts of India, while anger is still thought of as heat, it is a *dry* heat requiring lubrication.

Successful metaphors have to be both sufficiently ear-catching to take hold, but sufficiently ordinary to be acceptable. An organization might be called an octopus; most people know that an octopus has eight legs which reach out and cling and pull. But to call an organization a starfish or a squid would be unlikely to have the same effect, because people are less aware of how these animals behave.

But what about language itself? Metaphor has shaped, perhaps misshapen, our view of how it works. The most widely used metaphor is that of a game. Language has been likened to a game of chess, in which all the pieces are interdependent. The game image is useful. But like all metaphors it can be potentially misleading, in that any metaphor fits only partially. The game metaphor fits the rule-governed nature of language, but it perhaps over-estimates its neatness and tidiness. A more revealing image, now we understand the nature of language better, is that of the spider's web. The language web is potentially vast, though each language exploits only a small part of the available possibilities. Like the spider, we find that we don't need to cover the whole network of the web, but can narrow down the number of tracks we go along and select a few recurring routes. Ultimately, we must take care not to behave like the Chinese frog, which jumped back into its well because it couldn't stand the freedom outside.

Choosing the correct definition

1 Choose the best definition **A**, **B** or **C** for each of the words **1–10**.

1 subconsciously (line 8)

A without understanding why   **B** without talking about it   **C** without realizing it

2 merely (line 10)

A only   **B** sometimes   **C** in fact

3 notion (line 48)

A an idea   **B** an argument   **C** a contradiction

4 envisaged (line 57)

A explained in words   **B** shown in illustrations   **C** pictured in the mind

5 universal (line 73)

A found everywhere   **B** never changing   **C** found only in one place

6 ear-catching (line 77)

A loud enough to be heard
B repeated enough times to be familiar
C interesting enough to be noticed

7 shaped (line 87)

A confused   **B** enlarged   **C** influenced

8 likened (line 90)

A compared to   **B** made to seem like   **C** give as an example

9 partially (line 95)

A in some ways   **B** for those who like it   **C** if you believe in it

10 recurring (line 108)

A which repeats itself   **B** which we know   **C** which is successful

2 Look at the opening sentence of the article.

'Human beings can say what they want when they want, at least in theory.'

Discuss what change of meaning, if any, would result from using each of the listed alternatives instead of the given word in each case. Why did the writer choose the words above and not other similar words?

1 Human beings   **a** people   **4** what   **a** whatever
                       b men   **b** anything
                       c adults   **c** everything

2 can   **a** may   **5** want   **a** like
                       b could   **b** have to
                       c are able to   **c** need to

3 say   **a** talk about
                       b speak about
                       c communicate

3 What does the word 'they' in the opening sentence refer to? Look at these other reference words from the text and decide what they refer to.

Example:

'they' (line 9) refers to *human*s – the subject of the sentence.

'the latter' (line 16) refers to the second question at the end of the first paragraph, i.e. *the possibility that different languages reflect different ways of seeing the world.*

1	which (line 30)	**6**	their (line 69)
2	this (line 40)	**7**	it (line 88)
3	they (line 48)	**8**	it (line 93)
4	this (line 57)	**9**	its (line 98)
5	such (line 63)	**10**	that (line 101)

GRAMMAR 1
The passive

1 Look at this sentence from the article.

It has been suggested that powerful mental images may be created and preserved by metaphors.

2 Underline the verbs in the sentence which are in the passive.

3 Rewrite the sentence so that all the verbs are in the active voice.

4 Compare the two sentences. Why did the writer choose the passive for this sentence?

5 Look back at the article. Find other examples of the passive and decide why it has been used in each case.

📖 N.B. The Workbook has further work on the passive.

SPEAKING 2
Expressing time

1 Look at this phrase from the reading passage.

They stayed 10 days.

How is this phrase translated into your first language? Is the idea of time expressed in the same way as in English or differently?

2 How does your language express these times, in the same way as English or in other ways?

a week	a morning	an evening	a fortnight
an afternoon	a night	a weekend	

HELP WITH TALKING ABOUT PHOTOGRAPHS

Throughout this book there are a number of photographs for you to talk about related to the theme of the unit. It is important that as you prepare for Paper Five you get used to talking about a picture in the way that is expected in the exam. The questions on page 47 will help you.

A

B

■**1** Decide who is Student A and who is Student B and look at one of the two pictures labelled **A** or **B**.

As you look at the picture, think of the answer to these questions. Tell your partner about the picture, using the questions and the language in the box to help you structure what you say. Talk for about a minute while your partner listens.

The people:
> Who is it/are they?
> age/sex/physical appearance/dress
> job/relationship to place/others
> What (s)he is doing?
> attitude/feelings

The setting:
> Where is it?
> indoors/room/furniture/decorations
> outside/weather/time/season/buildings/
> vegetation/natural features
> city/country/part of world/Britain/your
> country?

The details:
> What is in the foreground?
> interesting details/objects/
> anything strange/anything typical

The context:
> What has just happened?
> What is just about to happen?

The theme:
> What does it make you think of?
> Why was the picture taken?
> What message does it convey?
> Where might you expect to find it?

It looks as if/though
(s)he looks + adjective
(s)he seems/appears to be + adjective
(s)he seems/appears to be + verb + *-ing*
I get the impression that (s)he is...
Maybe/perhaps (s)he is...
(s)he could/may/might be
(s)he must/can't be
It looks like + (a) noun

■**2** Look at your partner's picture. Think of some more personal questions you can ask related to the theme of the photograph, that could lead the discussion further without repeating what your partner has already said. Think about:

- his workspace
- his attitude to reading
- his taste in books/pictures/posters/magazines, etc.
- his typing/handwriting/word-processing skills
- his attitude to (un)tidiness
- his attitude towards issues raised in the picture
- attitudes to the issue in his country/ Britain/USA, etc.

■**3** In the examination, you may be asked to talk about one, two or three pictures. You may have two pictures to compare and contrast, for example. Use the language in the box to help you compare and contrast the pictures labelled **A** and **B**.

In this picture there's... whereas/while in this one there's...

Whereas/while this person looks..., this one looks more...

Whereas/while they both... only this one...

This one, on the other hand, looks...

Compared to that picture, this one is more...

They differ in terms of...

📖 N.B. The Workbook has further work on comparison and contrast.

▭ LISTENING 1

Selecting an answer

1 Discuss these questions with your partner.

Do you often read books in translation?

Are most major works of fiction from other languages translated into your language?

Which important writers from your country are translated into other languages?

Have you ever read a book in both your own language and in English? What did you think of the translation?

2 You will hear two parts of a radio discussion on the subject of books which are international bestsellers. Listen to Part One. For each of the questions **1–6**, mark each box **T** or **F** to show whether the statement is true or false.

1 Elizabeth recommends which new English books should be translated into foreign languages.   **1** ☐

2 Elizabeth chooses five or six books for each publisher.   **2** ☐

3 Elizabeth admits to trying to influence the publishers' final choice.   **3** ☐

4 Elizabeth chooses books that are already selling well in Britain.   **4** ☐

5 Elizabeth tries to avoid books which have had good reviews.   **5** ☐

6 Elizabeth believes that personal recommendations lead to most book sales.   **6** ☐

3 Listen to Part Two and for each of the questions **1–7**, mark each box **A** or **D** to show whether the two guests agree or disagree.

1 The need to explain things clearly for the benefit of foreign readers.   **1** ☐

2 The acceptability of English humour to foreign readers.   **2** ☐

3 The extent to which writers should consider their readers as they write.   **3** ☐

4 The attitude of American publishers.   **4** ☐

5 The lesson to be learnt from literary classics.   **5** ☐

6 The attitude of British and American readers to books in translation.   **6** ☐

7 The growth in popularity of translated novels in the UK.   **7** ☐

4   Imagine you have been asked to check a translation from your language into English. The translation has been done by a young inexperienced translator.

- What type of vocabulary mistakes would you expect to find in the translation?
- What type of grammar mistakes would you expect to find in the translation?
- What other type of mistakes do speakers of your language commonly make when translating into English?

5   How can you make sure that you do not make these mistakes in your own writing?

PHRASAL VERBS 1

Look at each of these phrases or sentences from the listening text. Each one contains a phrasal verb. Underline the phrasal verb in each example and then choose the best definition **A**, **B** or **C**.

1   Mervyn's latest novel has really taken off internationally.

   A been successful
   B been released
   C been removed

2   A new international market for books is opening up.

   A being offered
   B becoming accessible
   C gaining acceptability

3   The very same books are taken up by almost all my publishers.

   A adopted
   B translated
   C recommended

4   A lot of authors toss in local references which are meaningless to people in other countries.

   A include intentionally
   B include disrespectfully
   C include casually

5   American publishers will pick you up on the smallest point.

   A reject you
   B question you
   C criticise you

6   A good translator will sort out those little problems for readers in other languages.

   A rearrange
   B clarify
   C omit

Expressing likes and dislikes

1   Talk to your partner about a book you have bought, read or used recently which you found particularly enjoyable, useful or interesting.

2   Look at the types of book in the box and say which three you buy, read or use most regularly and why.

cookery books	(auto)biography	thrillers/crime novels
modern literature	science fiction	educational books
manuals	romantic novels	travel books
puzzle books	classic literature	reference books

3   What type of person do you think buys which type of book?

4   Which type of book do you think is the most popular in your country?

Comprehension

1   Look at the headline of the article on page 51. What do you think the article will say about book buying in Britain?

2   Read the article quickly to find out what the following numbers refer to:

95,000   899   35   55
55,000   12   793   47   22

3   Now read again more carefully and answer these questions.

1   Why has the writer used the expression 'chapters ahead'? (lines 2–3)

2   In your own words explain the term 'for pleasure'. (line 7)

3   What does 'the same' in line 14 refer to?

4   What does the word 'markedly' in line 15 mean?

5   What does 'the figure' in line 18 refer to?

6   What are 'culinary titles'? (line 25)

7   What does the phrasal verb 'bore out' in lines 31–32 mean?

8   Explain in your own words why 'trophy books' may be 'more purchased than read'. (lines 37/39)

9   What does 'they' in line 50 refer to?

10   What do you understand by the adverb 'steadily'? (line 58)

11   Explain in your own words the term 'consumer spending'. (lines 62–63)

12   Which word is used in the article for the conclusions drawn from the information collected in the survey?

The Joy of Reading Leaves Men on the Shelf

When it comes to reading habits, women are chapters ahead of men, a survey reveals today. The study of what Britons read – and when – found that 35% of men had not read a book for pleasure for five years or more, compared to only one in five women.

10 The survey, conducted by Book Marketing Ltd, also reveals that while 47% of women claimed to have finished a book in the previous fortnight, only 30% of men could say the same. Reading habits differ markedly with age; whereas only 18% of those aged 15 to 24 had read a book in the week before they were questioned, the figure for people aged between 25 and 34 was 21%, and 41% for those over 55.

20 Cookery books, with many titles linked to a television series, are the most popular type of book bought, although romantic fiction and puzzle books have the biggest volume of sales.

For example, culinary titles were bought by 21% of those who purchased a book compared to 18% who bought a crime story or thriller, 12% who bought a romantic novel and 7% who bought a work of 20th-century 30 fiction. A quick look around London book stores yesterday bore out some of the findings, with a range of cookery books, romantic works and thrillers on the best-seller racks. Also selling well were novels that had won literary prizes and what one bookseller called 'trophy' books, titles which look good on the bookshelf, but which tend to be more purchased than read.

40 The finding that women are greater readers than men was supported by a quick survey of book buyers by this newspaper. 'I think it's because women are continually trying to change and improve themselves, and are more flexible and open to new experiences,' Liz Kay, a curator at the Tate Gallery, said. Tamsin Summerson, 22, said she was aware of the difference among her friends. 'If you ask a man what book they've just 50 read, they're likely to have forgotten or they will change the subject. On the other hand, with a woman, you're likely to get into a lengthy discussion about it.'

But whichever sex you are, it is getting harder to be well-read. The number of books published in Britain has risen steadily in recent years, from just under 55,000 in 1987 to just over 95,000 today. Book prices have also risen from an average of 60 £7.93 for a novel in 1991 compared with £8.99 today. Consumer spending on books has jumped from £755 million in 1985 to £1673 million.

Complex sentences: Comparison and contrast

▬ **1** Look at the first sentence in the second paragraph of the article.

1 How many pieces of information does the sentence give?

2 Which word provides the link between the two main parts of the sentence?

3 How is the punctuation of the sentence important?

4 Why has the writer chosen this type of sentence to present the information?

▬ **2** Look at the next two sentences in the article. Which words provide the link between the two main parts of these sentences? Are they making the same type of link?

📖 N.B. The Workbook has further work on this type of sentence.

Constructing a questionnaire

1 The article talks about two surveys. How are the two surveys different? Why do you think the newspaper decided to carry out the second survey?

2 Look at the article. What questions did the Book Marketing Survey ask people? Make a list. What order do you think the questions were asked in? Why?

3 What questions did the newspaper survey ask people?

4 Do you think a survey of people in your country/school would find the same results as the two surveys in the article? Why (not)?

5 Design a questionnaire about the type of recorded music people buy. Your questionnaire should be quite short so that you can ask lots of people (i.e. about 8-12 questions) and should provide you with the following information to present in a magazine article:

- information about the people asked

- statistical information

- some subjective opinions

LISTENING 2
Multiple choice

1 What are the qualities of a good novel? Talk about:

> plot   characterization   descriptions   tension   humour   style of writing

2 You will hear an interview with a novelist who has written a book called 'The Secrets of Best-seller Writing'. For each of the questions **1–6**, choose the answer **A**, **B**, **C** or **D** which you think fits best according to what you hear.

1 Why did she refuse initially to write the book?

A She was busy writing something else.
B She found this sort of book irritating.
C Other books on the subject were rubbish.
D Other writers would probably want to write it.

2 She feels that books advising writers are often misleading with regard to

A the nature of the readership.
B the quality of the product.
C the importance of reviews.
D the attitude of the book business.

3 How did she feel about the number of people attending her talk at the book fair?

A disappointed
B surprised
C gratified
D nervous

4 John Grisham serves as an example of how

A you can't teach people to write.
B you can't predict who will be successful.
C one successful writer benefited from advice.
D some people dream of writing a best-seller.

5 What must all writers have before they can begin to write a best-seller?

A an outline of the plot
B a narrative instinct
C some clear literary ideals
D a true story as a base

6 Why does she feel that, as a novelist, she never gets 'writer's block'?

A She has great self-discipline.
B She has a fixed daily routine.
C She's always found writing easy.
D She trained in another field.

Defining words and phrases

Look at these sentences which are taken from the listening texts. Explain in your own words what you think each of the underlined words and expressions means. The first one has been done for you as an example.

0 The book tells you how to write a <u>smash hit</u>.

A smash hit is something, like a book or a recording, which sells lots of copies.

1 The <u>heady summit</u> of an author's ambition.

2 There's a lot of advice which <u>boils down to</u> 'write a bad book'.

3 We can <u>take it as read</u> that there's a demand for a book like this, can't we?

4 I recently did a talk where <u>would-be</u> authors could come and ask for advice.

5 The event was <u>packed to the gills</u> and they actually had to <u>turn people away</u>.

6 Is there not a sense in which you are <u>pedalling day dreams</u>?

7 If you picked any <u>buttoned-down</u> young lawyer in the Mid-west.

8 I'm a <u>sucker</u> for a good story.

9 A friend of mine gave me the <u>germ</u> of the story.

10 You should <u>map it all out</u> in advance and know where you are going.

11 Don't <u>hamper</u> your writing with literary ideals that you may have picked up.

12 Writers sometimes get into <u>sloughs of despond</u>.

Similes

1 When people or things are likened to other things this is called a simile.

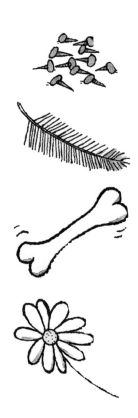

Example:
He's as deaf as a post.
The room was as cold as ice.

Match the beginnings of the simile in **A** with its conclusion in **B**.

	A	**B**
1	as light as	nails
2	as different as	life
3	as large as	a feather
4	as hard as	a pancake
5	as quick as	chalk and cheese
6	as flat as	a cucumber
7	as fresh as	a bone
8	as good as	a daisy
9	as cool as	a flash
10	as dry as	gold

2 Which of these similes would you use to talk about:

- people
- places
- objects

N.B. The Workbook has further work on similes.

Word families

Look at these groups of words connected with language. For each group decide what is the difference in meaning between each word. Use a dictionary if necessary.

1 linguistics, linguistic, linguist
2 vocabulary, dictionary
3 accent, dialect
4 translate, interpret
5 pronunciation, phonetics
6 literal, metaphorical, idiomatic
7 style, register
8 word, syllable, sentence, paragraph
9 stress, intonation
10 spelling, syntax

Cloze passage

1 What is Esperanto? What is the idea behind it? What languages is it based on?

Do you know any Esperanto? Do you know anybody who can speak it?

2 Fill each of the numbered blanks in the passage with **one** suitable word. The first one has been done for you as an example.

Esperanto

The best-known (**0**) __*of*__ all the artificial languages, Esperanto, was the invention of a Polish oculist, Ludwig Zamenhof. He made the first draft of his international language (**1**) _____ he was fifteen. (**2**) _____ own language background was very mixed: Russian was used at home, with Yiddish and Polish outside, and French, German, Latin, Greek and English taught in school.

The scheme was first published in Russian in 1887. The first Esperanto journal was published in 1889 and the first congress was (**3**) _____ in 1905, bringing (**4**) _____ nearly 700 delegates from 20 countries. Today Esperanto is frequently encountered (**5**) _____ international conferences. Several journals and newspapers are published in the language and (**6**) _____ is a large translated literature in (**7**) _____ to original work written in Esperanto.

(**8**) _____ its popularity, Esperanto has failed (**9**) _____ achieve official status as an international language. A proposal to the United Nations in 1966 was signed by nearly a million people from 74 countries, (**10**) _____ was not accepted. There is a lot of opposition from those (**11**) _____ favour English as a world language, and from supporters of other artificial languages.

Several criticisms have been (**12**) _____ of the language, but it is generally easy to learn to read Esperanto. (**13**) _____ always with language learning, (**14**) _____, passive competence is much easier to achieve than active use, and a (**15**) _____ deal of memory work is still needed before fluency is acquired.

WRITING 1
Giving opinions

1 Discuss these three questions with your partner.

1 What would be the advantages of having a universal language?

2 What problems would there be in choosing one language to use?

3 What problems would be involved in introducing a new artificial language like Esperanto?

2 Look at these comments made by English language students and tell your partner whether you agree or disagree with them.

a English is the world language and everyone should be able to speak it.

b English should be simplified; the grammar is too complicated, the spelling and pronunciation is illogical.

c We need to protect our own languages against English by not allowing advertisers and the media to use English words.

3 Read this composition title.

Many people say that there should be one universal language which everyone learns to speak. Some people favour an artificial language, like Esperanto, whilst others point to English as the logical choice. What are your views on the subject?

1 Now complete this outline plan of the composition.

Introduction
Need for a universal language
_____
_____
_____
Conclusion

2 Make notes for each paragraph, using the points from your discussion. Then compare your notes with your partner. Add any points you might have forgotten.

3 Look back at the grammar points in this unit and think how you might use them in your writing.

4 Look at the words and phrases in the box. Which of them would be suitable for use in a conclusion?

to sum up	in the final analysis	lastly	on balance	finally
last but not least	taking all the arguments into consideration			
to conclude	in the end	at the end of the day		

5 Write the introduction and conclusion of your composition. Then complete the other paragraphs, using your plan and notes.

1   In this section you must choose the word or phrase, **A**, **B**, **C** or **D**, which best completes each sentence.

1   Humans create their own limited mental pictures of the world which are _____ in language.

   A returned   **B** reflected   **C** reimbursed   **D** recruited

2   It has been suggested that powerful mental _____ may be created and preserved by metaphors.

   A figures   **B** statues   **C** dreams   **D** images

3   The Chinese frog jumped back into its well because it couldn't _____ the freedom outside.

   A cope   **B** struggle   **C** stand   **D** deal

4   Elizabeth is what is _____ as an international literary scout.

   A known   **B** called   **C** referred   **D** termed

5   Tell me, Elizabeth, what does your work _____ of?

   A contain   **B** consist   **C** compose   **D** contend

6   My job is to _____ potential best-sellers for translation.

   A touch   **B** pluck   **C** point   **D** spot

7   I've always written my novels with a _____ to their being read by people in different countries.

   A sight   **B** hope   **C** mind   **D** view

8   The survey was _____ by Book Marketing Ltd.

   A constituted   **B** conveyed   **C** conducted   **D** collected

9   I suppose we can take it as _____ that there's demand for a book like this, can't we?

   A right   **B** read   **C** said   **D** told

10   At first, I refused the offer because I was in the _____ of writing a novel.

   A middle   **B** core   **C** heart   **D** centre

2 Fill each of the numbered blanks in the passage with **one** suitable word.

Reaching out

The ability to read is for most of us like the taste of water in the mouth; we can't imagine (**1**) _____ life would be like without it. We are all, of course, (**2**) _____ of the predicament of the blind, but for many people (**3**) _____ is little understanding of the predicament of others for (**4**) _____ reading is a real problem – the deaf, for instance, or the dyslexic, or (**5**) _____ who for one reason or (**6**) _____ find it more difficult than we (**7**) _____ to comprehend the relationship (**8**) _____ symbols on paper and words (**9**) _____ the mind.

Unfortunately, until comparatively recently, lack (**10**) _____ knowledge, imagination and understanding has not only affected parents, (**11**) _____ extended to teachers and educationalists, with some very curious results. It is only in the past ten years, (**12**) ____ the use of sign language has (**13**) _____ a primary method of teaching deaf children. Previously, signing was discouraged on (**14**) _____ grounds that it set deaf children (**15**) _____ from their contemporaries in a way which might (**16**) _____ damaging.

Slowly, things are improving, (**17**) _____; not least through the work of the organization called REACH which strongly (**18**) _____ the case for special treatment for children with visual or other reading problems. REACH has devised several ways of working with teachers to single (**19**) _____ and help the average one in three children who will, (**20**) _____ some time, need special help from a parent or teacher.

3 Fill each of the blanks with a suitable word or phrase.
1 When he heard he'd won the prize Simon was overcome _____ emotion.
2 A dentist who is bad-tempered is not really cut _____ the job.
3 The more you talk about spiders, _____ nervous Marie gets.
4 I meant to pick up some bread at the supermarket, but I'm afraid it _____ my mind.
5 I wish people wouldn't smoke in restaurants, it really gets _____ nerves.

4 For each of the sentences below, write a new sentence as similar as possible in meaning to the original sentence, but using the word given. This word **must not be altered** in any way.

Example: A lot of people attended the meeting.

   turnout

Answer: There was a very good turnout for the meeting.

1 I always wanted to be a writer when I grew up.

ambition

_____

2 Why do you think your first novel was so successful?

account

_____

3 Whilst having an idealized notion of a week, people may organize their own lives quite differently.

although

_____

4 People have made a comparison between language and a game of chess.

likened

_____

5 Only part of the story he told was true.

partially

_____

6 Chris likes eating pizza a great deal.

fond

_____

7 I very rarely go into fast-food restaurants.

hardly

_____

8 Clare doesn't really like talking about her problem.

reluctant

_____

9 The origins of dental fear tend to be found in childhood.

originate

_____

10 It's not Jane's intention to forgive Peter for embarrassing her.

no

_____

5 Finish each of the following sentences in such a way that it is as similar as possible in meaning to the sentence printed before it.

Example: Immediately after his departure things improved.

Answer: No sooner *had he departed than things improved.*

1 The number of books published has risen steadily.
There has been _____

2 I found the things people said about best-sellers very irritating.
I was _____

3 They discussed the acceptability of English humour to foreign readers.
They discussed how _____

4 What are the chances of the book becoming a best-seller?
How likely _____

5 As soon as it was published in translation, the book became a best-seller.
No sooner _____

6 In time, unpicked fruit will rot and fall to the ground.
If _____

7 It's advisable for Rosemary to avoid drinking tea or coffee for a while.
Rosemary would _____

8 The growing of that type of plant in Europe dates back to at least 1839.
By 1840, _____

9 Richard didn't set out to cause an argument.
Richard had no _____

10 Elaine's membership of the Society dates back to 1984.
Elaine has _____

A Fine Romance

Talking about photographs

1 Look at the photographs and talk to your partner about:

1 the relationships between the people and how the people are feeling:

- about themselves
- about others
- about what they are doing

2 what they are thinking about

3 what type of person you think each one is:

- what qualities they have
- what failings they have

2 Which of these characteristics would you like your ideal person to have? Choose the five most important. Tell your partner why.

modesty	loyalty	honesty	generosity	reliability
style	intelligence	bravery	judgement	patience
charm	sense of humour	faithfulness	sociability	talent
caution	resourcefulness	taste	common sense	beauty

3 Think about your ideal/perfect partner in life. Talk about what is important to you and why.

Physical appearance:
Height, weight, colouring, age, health and fitness, etc.

Status:
Money, social position, occupation, family background, education, etc.

Character:
Qualities and failings that matter.

Which would affect your choice most?

4 Is your perfect partner similar to you or different to you? Is this significant?

Do men and women have different ideas of what makes a good partner?

5 With your partner, look at this advertisement for an introductions agency. Talk about:

- What it is
- How it works
- What sort of people use them
- Whether you think they are successful

HAPPY HEARTS INTRODUCTION AGENCY

♥

Find your perfect partner in life

♥

Our database holds details of 2000 single people

♥

All areas, all ages, all interests catered for

♥

Confidentiality guaranteed

6 Look at the three passages. Each one is connected with dating agencies. For each one, talk about:

- where you might find a passage like this;
- who it is talking to;
- the style it is written in;
- what you think about what it is saying.

A The Happy Hearts Introductions Agency is designed for individuals seeking a genuine one-to-one relationship. Clients are reminded that entries will not be accepted on to our database if they state a race, creed, colour or nationality in the person sought and that all entries must be within the law. The Agency reserves the right, therefore, to exercise its own discretion in refusing any entries which may give offence or be in any way unlawful.

B *Hi. Tall, slim and exceptionally attractive. I'm a struggling musician who travels a great deal and has many friends. By nature, I'm caring and affectionate with a good sense of humour. Being very sociable, I have a tendency to throw impromptu parties. My ideal partner is someone who is tolerant enough to put up with my unpredictable lifestyle, but brave enough to stand up to me sometimes. It's someone who will be there when I need them, but who will also leave me the space when I need to be by myself.*

C Once you've selected your ideal partner from our shortlist, naturally you'll be keen to get in touch with them. You can write a letter or e-mail to your chosen person through us, using the database code number on the printout. It couldn't be easier, and there's no need to give your personal details if you don't want to. Sooner or later, if you hit it off, you may want to actually meet your new friend. Remember this is up to you to decide; there's no pressure. But when you go to meet the person for the first time, we suggest you:

- tell a friend of your plans
- always meet in a public place
- don't give your address or phone number unless you're sure you want to continue with the relationship

7 Write either:

Your own (real or imaginary) entry for the agency's database.
Your reply to the person who wrote passage B.

Remember that you have to describe yourself in a flattering light and give a good idea of the qualities you are looking for in a perfect partner.

▭ LISTENING 1

Selecting an answer

1 You will hear a reading from a novel in which a woman is remembering her first romantic encounter as a teenager. For questions **1–7**, mark each box **T** or **F** to show whether the statement is true or false.

1 Sylvia first became interested in Robert because of his name.   1 ☐

2 Jenny probably told Robert that Sylvia liked him.   2 ☐

3 Sylvia was, on balance, pleased to receive the letter.   3 ☐

4 Sylvia regretted declining Robert's invitation.   4 ☐

5 Sylvia was annoyed about the rumours Jenny spread.   5 ☐

6 Sylvia was concerned about other people's opinion of Robert.   6 ☐

7 Sylvia found Robert uninteresting.   7 ☐

2 Listen again and note down what you have learnt about the characters of Sylvia, Jenny and Robert.

Multiple choice

1 Read this continuation of Sylvia's story.

Robert Kett was hanging about a little way down the road from our house, pretending to be doing something to his bike. If I had not recognized him, I would have recognized his bike anywhere, a birthday present from his parents whose perception of their son clearly differed from my own. It was blue and white with turned down handlebars and the lines of a cheetah poised to spring upon an unsuspecting gazelle. Not that I had seen – nor ever expected to see – Robert Kett riding it with the panache it deserved. He seemed happiest quietly
10 pushing it along, himself padding alongside in a submissive way that did not make it entirely clear which of the two was in charge.

We said hello to each other and were, as usual, immediately, at a loss for words. I think I said something about liking his pullover, which was a dazzling new white, hand-knitted one in cable-stitch. Going bright red – when it came to blushing there was not much to choose between us – he told me his Aunt Mabel had knitted it for him. To break the painful silence which followed this information I mentioned that I was on the way to feed a donkey. I was not conscious of framing this comment in the form of
20 an invitation, but he took it as one, and I did not contradict him; it was such a relief to discover a purpose for our being together.

We walked in a depressive quiet down to the cross-roads. I had long ago resigned myself to the sad recognition that – in the circles I frequented at any rate – people did not converse with either the wit or the high seriousness they invariably exhibited in books. Even so, with nothing but Aunt Mabel's pullover between us and silence, I could not help feeling that we had touched rock bottom. Once we got into the back path things got even worse. Robert Kett grew fussy and I could never abide fussiness. It seemed that none of the householders cared a great deal about the state of the hedges which flanked the path, for with spring passing into summer, the wild roses had grown
30 prodigiously, the brambles arching over the pathway or snaking thornily along the ground with the express aim, surely, of tripping up the unsuspecting passer-by. As a place for picking up scratches on the beautiful blue and white enamel of a new bike, it took a lot of beating. Much as I hated fuss, I felt sufficient sympathy for my companion in his obvious distress to suggest that he and his bicycle change their minds about accompanying me further and retreat to the safety of made-up roads. Robert Kett's refusal to withdraw may have demonstrated a gratifying desire for my company despite all danger, if only he had not said: 'It's ages since I saw a donkey.'

Robert Kett and the donkey liked each other instantly. It was love at first sight. My titular boyfriend took to the donkey in a way I had never seen him take to me.
40 Undaunted by the large yellow teeth that made me prefer to throw bread down in the ground rather than risk my fingers, Robert fearlessly held out lumps of bread for the animal to snuffle up with its slobbery lips. He patted Bagshaw, for that was the donkey's name, on the muzzle like an old friend, shooed the flies away from his eyes and even snagged his new pullover on the barbed wire and didn't seem to care.

If I was, to be honest, a little put out by this level of vivacity, never triggered by my presence, it was as nothing to my annoyance at Bagshaw's response. Here was I who

had been feeding the wretched beast day after day without receiving as much as a hee-haw in return, and here was a complete stranger moving in effortlessly to
50 take over the heart which should, if there were any justice in the world, belong to me. Bagshaw purred, Bagshaw simpered, Bagshaw fluttered his long eyelashes at Robert Kett in a way that was quite disgusting. I might as well have not been there at all. 'It takes one donkey to recognize another', I thought ferociously, but I remained uncomforted. My faithless lover then turned to me and demanded 'Is that all there is?' Though the answer must have been plain to see – where, for heaven's sake, did he think I kept extra
60 bread? I burst into tears.

I don't know which of us was the most embarrassed – me, Robert Kett or the donkey, but only the latter had the sense to do something about it. Pushing his head even further than usual through the strands of barbed wire, he first rubbed his nose affectionately against Robert's new pullover, then, opening his mouth wide, champed his teeth with an audible 'clack' down on Aunt Mabel's handiwork and bit a large piece out of it.

70 It was masterly done. The shock of it dried my tears instantly. The destruction so utter as to preclude pettifogging worries about whether or not the damage could be repaired. Even as the boy stood staring down unbelievingly at his front, the nothingness enlarged itself. It seemed that breathing was enough to send more stitches into oblivion, more wool unravelling, more cables untwisting themselves.

When Robert Kett demanded in a high-pitched voice, ' What am I going to tell Auntie?' I took charge,
80 the way, it seemed to me, girls often had to when faced with boys' inability to cope. 'Tell her you lost it. She'll knit you another. Women always buy more wool than they need, she'll be glad of a reason to use it up. Red with the effort of stifling my laughter, I helped Robert Kett divest himself of the mangled remains of his pullover – not easy because some of the loose strands of wool had wound themselves around the buttons of the shirt he wore underneath.

'Hang on a moment.' I said as I pressed close against
90 his chest working at getting the buttons free. I hadn't heard footsteps or the gate opening, but suddenly I heard Miss Locke's voice inquiring icily: 'What on earth is going on?'

From *The Quivering Tree*

1 How did Sylvia regard Robert's bicycle?
   A She longed to be able to ride it.
   B She felt it was unsuited to him.
   C She admired his choice of model.
   D She was unused to seeing him with it.

2 How did Sylvia feel when Robert said he would like to come with her to see the donkey?
   A she was embarrassed
   B she felt relieved
   C she was disappointed
   D she felt confused

3 What annoyed Sylvia most as they walked along together?
   A the topic of conversation
   B Robert's fears for his bicycle
   C the state of the pathway
   D her inability to change the subject

4 Why did Sylvia get so upset when Robert met the donkey?
   A She felt betrayed by Robert.
   B She felt excluded.
   C She felt jealous of the donkey.
   D She felt foolish.

5 How did Sylvia feel about the damage to the pullover?
   A She thought it insignificant.
   B She found it amusing.
   C She felt sorry for Robert.
   D She felt angry with the donkey.

Part Two
Comprehension

1 Now look back carefully at the text to find these words and phrases.

1 What word(s) could be used as a synonym of 'panache'? (line 9)

2 Who are 'the two' referred to in line 11?

3 What does 'at a loss for words' in line 14 mean?

4 What does Sylvia mean by the phrase 'there was not much to choose between us'? (lines 16–17)

5 Explain what you understand by the term 'depressive quiet'. (line 22)

6 What does Sylvia mean by 'the circles I frequented'? (line 23)

7 What is meant by the phrase 'we had touched rock bottom'? (line 26)

8 What is meant by the phrase 'it took a lot of beating'? (line 33)

9 Why does Sylvia describe Robert as her 'titular' boyfriend? (line 39)

10 What does 'put out' in line 45 mean?

11 What does 'all' in line 57 refer to?

12 What does 'the latter' in line 63 refer to?

13 What does 'it' in line 70 refer to?

14 What doe you think 'pettifogging' in line 72 means?

15 What does Sylvia mean by 'the nothingness'? (line 74)

2 Now answer these questions.

1 What more have you learnt about the characters of Sylvia and Robert? At the end of the extract who do you feel more sympathy for? Why?

2 What are Sylvia's strengths and qualities? What are her failings?

3 Who do you think Miss Locke is? Why do you think she is 'icy'?

GRAMMAR 1
Narrative devices

1 Look at these beginnings of sentences:

- *Undaunted by the yellow teeth, Robert …*
- *Pushing his head through the barbed wire, Bagshaw …*
- *No sooner had he seen the donkey, than Robert …*
- *Unlike many animals, donkeys …*
- *Surprised as Sylvia was, she was able to …*

2 Complete each of the sentences in the context of the story.

3 How and why are these types of sentence useful when telling a story?

📖 N.B. The Workbook has further work on narrative devices.

Narratives

In the examination you are often asked to write a narrative composition. You may be given the first or last line of a story and asked to write the rest. Had Sylvia's story about the donkey been an exam question, it might have read:

Write a story ending in the words 'I suddenly heard a voice behind me inquiring icily; *'What on earth is going on?'*

Before beginning a narrative composition, it is important to think about:

- the plot;
- the characters;
- from whose point of view the story is told.

1 Look back at Sylvia's story and put these narrative points in order.

Sylvia feels betrayed

A decision is reached

Robert's true motive revealed

Sylvia leads Robert into danger

Caught in the act

An awkward meeting

Bagshaw rescues the situation

Love at first sight

Sylvia sees Robert with his bicycle

Sylvia takes charge

2 Talk to your partner about the advantages and disadvantages of stories told in the:

- first person
- third person

3 How would the story be different if Robert had written it? Talk to your partner about Robert's attitude towards:

- the bicycle
- the pullover
- Sylvia
- the donkey

4 Write a short version (about 350 words) of the story written from Robert's point of view.

Note completion

▓ 1 What sort of things cause arguments in a relationship? Talk about:

| friends | different interests | family | work | moods | money |

▓ 2 Are arguments in a relationship a good thing or a bad thing?

▓ 3 You will hear a speaker from the Marriage Guidance Organization talking about the type of problems it helps couples with. For questions **1–10**, complete the notes with a word or short phrase.

Marriage Guidance Organization

Number of new couples the organization helps per year: _____ **1**

Peak time for requests for help: _____ **2**

Two fundamental types of couple: parallel and _____ **3**

Two types of parallel couple:

A power couple:

- both partners focused on careers

- both partners used to being _____ **4**

- couple not used to being _____ **5**

B traditional couple:

- woman focused on _____ **6**

- man focused on _____ **7**

Advice to both types of parallel couple. Need to _____ **8**

Advice to power couples. Consider _____ **9**

Advice to traditional couples. Consider going _____ **10**

▓ 4 Do you agree that arguments are more likely on holiday? Tell your partner about arguments you have had or witnessed in similar situations.

Cloze passage

1 Fill each of the numbered blanks in the passage with **one** suitable word from the box.

The first one has been done for you as an example.

behind	but	care	goes	in	into	it
of	or	around	with	the	there	something
us	when	which	will	matter	turns	~~because~~

How do you row?

Rows are inevitable in a relationship. A row occurs (**0**) __*because*__ two individuals are not the same. No (**1**) _____ how close you are, there (**2**) _____ be conflicts unless you are in (**3**) _____ first throes of love – which, you have to admit, is a temporary illness, during (**4**) _____ you subsume yourself to the relationship and don't (**5**) _____ which film you see.

(**6**) _____ private we've all experienced it. It's the moment (**7**) _____ sheer frustration rises to the surface, and dignity (**8**) _____ into free-fall. Most of (**9**) _____ have had the heated slanging match full (**10**) _____ bile and vitriol, name-calling and offensive personal criticism. Often (**11**) _____ starts quite trivially: in the supermarket over which brand of toothpaste to buy, (**12**) _____ on a night out over which type of restaurant to eat in. A lover's tiff is painful enough (**13**) _____ closed doors, but when your row (**14**) _____ into a public spectacle, it's humiliating.

If you don't row, there's probably (**15**) _____ wrong. You may manage to steer your way (**16**) _____ conflicts most of the time, (**17**) _____ inevitably when you are tired or stressed, (**18**) _____ is a head-on collision. Here is our psychologist's guide to the roles we take when we row, together (**19**) _____ some tips in case your partner falls (**20**) _____ one of the categories.

2 Look back at the text. In your own words explain what these words and phrases mean.

1 slanging match
2 first throes
3 free-fall
4 lover's tiff
5 name-calling
6 bile and vitriol
7 sheer

3 Talk to your partner about a time when you had either a lover's tiff or a slanging match. How did you feel: before? during? afterwards?

Matching

■ 1 Look at the words in the box. They each describe a type of role people adopt
when they row. Read some more of the text and match each description to its
title by writing one of the words from the box in each space.

Bullies Weepers Dramatists Sulkers
Revengers Screamers Slow-burners

Which type are you?

a _____ find that words don't work for them, so they resort to violence. Until
children learn to talk, they express themselves physically by grabbing things – and these
people haven't learnt that adults can't get away with that. Education gives access to power
through words; uneducated people tend to be more violent.

b _____ make a mountain out of a molehill. They feel that they are not being
taken seriously, so they have to exaggerate their emotion. They couldn't get their own way
as children, so they became manipulative and scheming. They cry wolf to get what they want.

c _____ fear they will lose the argument if they let you be heard, possibly
because they came from a large family where they had to make a lot of noise to be heard.
They are insecure and may have a short fuse.

d _____ are depressive types, prone to rumination, who nurse their self-hatred.
They feel misunderstood and turn their aggression against themselves. As children they
probably thought their siblings had a better deal. 'It's not fair' is the typical refrain of this
type, who feel powerless and have given up trying to get their point across.

e _____ go for the sympathy vote. They were abandoned a lot as children. Now
as soon as they start to get angry, they feel sad too. In childhood this may have been a
successful tactic in gaining sympathy, particularly if they were attractive – who can resist a
tearfully cute baby. It worked then and they are still trying it now.

f _____ are envious. When they were three years old they weren't just quietly
jealous of their brother's or sister's toy, they would go and destroy it. If someone else has
anything they want – be it physical or emotional – they are liable to damage it. If they think
something bad has happened to them, they can't let it go. If they think someone has
something better than they have, they want to spoil the other person's prize.

g _____ are passive-aggressive. They don't express aggression when they feel it,
or when provoked, but it builds up and then comes out as a disastrous explosion. It can
take a lot to get them wound up – they are not provoked by what annoys most people – but
they can be cold, and inflict pain without regard.

2 Here are some tips that the psychologist gave to anyone whose partner fell into one of the categories. Which tip do you think matches which of the types?

> *Psychologist's Tips*
>
> - Try to take them out of themselves, get them to open up.
> - Hide your kitchen knives.
> - Be calm and firm. Don't be a victim.
> - Give them a Kleenex tissue and tell them to grow up.
> - Find a way to give vent to their creative side.
> - Tell them they'll succeed by reason, not volume.
> - Hide your most treasured possessions and feelings.

3 Do you recognize any of the types of personality described? In yourself? In other people you know?

4 Is it better to have rows with family and friends or is it better to try and avoid them? Are there good and bad times to start a row? Should you intervene to try and stop two other people rowing?

5 Explain in your own words what these words and expressions from the text mean.

1 resort to
2 cry wolf
3 a short fuse
4 siblings
5 tactic
6 liable to
7 wound up
8 take them out of themselves
9 give vent

PHRASAL VERBS 1

1 Look at these two phrases from the article. Underline the phrasal verbs in each one.

These people haven't learnt that adults can't get away with that.
They've given up trying to get their point across.

2 Complete each sentence with a suitable preposition.

1 After that big argument, John and Barbara got on much better _____ each other.

2 The argument began when Julie said that Tom was always trying to get _____ of doing the washing-up.

3 I enjoy writing letters, but I'm so busy that I never get _____ to it.

4 Mrs Black was never sure what her children were getting _____ to when she wasn't watching them.

5 'How are you getting _____ with your homework, David?' said his father.

Discussing proverbs

■ **1** Look at these proverbs and common expressions. With your partner decide:

- what each one means
- if a similar saying is used in your language

A Leave no stone unturned
B Honesty is the best policy
C Don't beat about the bush
D Pride comes before a fall
E Once upon a time
F Attack is the best form of defence
G Don't hide your light under a bushel
H Many a true word is said in jest
I Keep your eye on the ball
J Make a clean breast of it

■ **2** Look at this magazine feature about how to win an argument. Do you agree with the points made?

HOW TO WIN AN ARGUMENT

1 Prepare. Preparation is the key. Understand all the facets of your argument, and your opponent's.

2 Empower yourself. Everyone is capable of making the winning argument. Self-belief is utterly convincing.

3 Relate your argument in the form of an example. Traditionally, we are tellers of tales and listeners. Use this familiar format to express your ideas.

4 Tell the truth. Establish your credibility from the start. With credibility comes trust.

5 State objectives clearly. If you want something, ask for it. Don't let others misinterpret your requests.

6 Avoid sarcasm, scorn and ridicule. Use humour cautiously. Give respect to your opponent. Nobody admires the scoffer, the cynic, the mocker. Humour, when properly used, can be devastating, but beware, badly used, it can backfire catastrophically!

7 Logic is power. If you have logic on your side, ride it for all it's worth and don't allow yourself to be distracted by red herrings. It may not always be fun, but logic is powerful.

8 Act to win. Don't go on the defensive. Take the initiative. Take control.

9 Admit the weaknesses of your argument at the beginning. You can expose your weak points better than your opponent, who will always expose them in the darkest possible way.

10 Understand your power and your argument. With proper understanding you give yourself permission to win. But remember, arrogance, insolence and stupidity are close relatives.

■ **3** Decide which of the sayings or proverbs **A–J** matches each piece of advice **1–10**.

LISTENING 3

Sentence completion

1 Look at this short passage. Read it quietly to yourself, thinking about where you might find it and the style in which it is written as well as the content.

> The romance between a young fireman and his ex-girlfriend was rekindled when he was called to a fire at her house. Richard Lightfoot and Donna Perry had split up two months previously and had not spoken to each other since. But in response to a 999 call at four in the morning, Mr Lightfoot found himself in front of his ex-girlfriend's burning flat and smashed his way in to rescue her. 'He was a real hero and saved my life,' said Ms Parry, 'a bit like James Bond.'

2 What do you understand by the phrase 'madly in love'? Do you think it is possible to measure the intensity of love? What sort of criteria would be useful for determining how deeply in love people might be? What questions could you ask them, what tests could you run?

3 You will hear part of a talk by a scientist on the subject of the power of love. For questions **1–11**, complete the sentences with a word or short phrase.

The power of love

The speaker quotes poets who describe the power of love as [_____ **1**].

When two people are 'madly in love', their [_____ **2**] may become linked together.

In the first part of Grinberg's experiment, volunteer couples looked at each other, but didn't [_____ **3**].

The Faraday Cage is designed so that [_____ **4**] between people is impossible.

Grinberg's subjects wore [_____ **5**] which measured their brain waves.

Similar brain patterns were recorded between partners who also exhibited the greatest level of [_____ **6**].

The speaker doubts that the results can be explained in terms of [_____ **7**] by scientists.

Another possible explanation, rejected by the speaker, is that the experiments were not [_____ **8**].

One interpretation of Grinberg's findings is that the mind may be located [_____ **9**].

One implication of Grinberg's work is that people may need to be more careful about their [_____ **10**].

Dr Grinberg feels that it's important for people to have [_____ **11**] in business, schools and the family.

4 Look at this excerpt from the listening. Complete the passage with a word from the box; some words can be used more than once. Then listen again to check.

there	this	three	these	first	them
their	second	that	who	third	

(**0**) ___*There*___ are only (**1**) _____ explanations for the results of (**2**) _____ experiments. The (**3**) _____ is a deliberate hoax by the scientists. (**4**) _____ seems extremely unlikely knowing (**5**) _____ academic background. The (**6**) _____ is (**7**) _____ the volunteers were communicating by some conventional means, (**8**) _____ is (**9**) _____ the experiments were not properly conducted. (**10**) _____ also seems very unlikely as the experiments were very carefully set up by experienced scientists (**11**) _____ had repeated (**12**) _____ many times with many different subjects. The (**13**) _____ possibility is (**14**) _____ some brains can communicate in an as yet unknown way.

WRITING 2

Summary

Complete this summary of how the experiment was conducted, using your own words.

First of all, _____

_____

_____

After that, _____

_____

_____

Then, _____

_____

_____

In conclusion, _____

_____

_____

HELP WITH USE OF ENGLISH: TRANSFORMATIONS 1

■ 1 Parts of the Use of English paper asks you to transform sentences from one structure to another. In Paper 3, Question 2 you are given a complete sentence.

Example: I expect that he will get there by lunchtime.

This is followed by an incomplete sentence.

Answer: I expect him _____ .

The example needs to be completed like this:

Answer: I expect him *to get there by lunchtime.*

The new sentence must have a similar meaning to the original one, but will probably use a different grammatical structure. Other changes may also be necessary to complete the new sentence.

■ 2 Look at this transformation.

Example: 'I'll certainly meet you at the airport tomorrow', said my uncle.

Answer: My uncle promised *to meet me at the airport the next day.*

What has changed? Why?
What has remained the same? Why?
What has been omitted?
What has been added
Are there any other correct ways to complete the transformation?

■ 3 Are these examples of good transformations?

Example: She was surprised that the tickets were so expensive.

a She found it *surprising that the tickets were so expensive.*

b She found it *a surprise that the tickets were not cheap.*

a is a good transformation because the new sentence has the same meaning as the original sentence.

b is incorrect because the expression *She found it* is followed by an *-ing* form, and *not cheap* does not have the same meaning as *so expensive.*

Example: Sid tried to explain how the machine works, but his colleagues didn't understand.

a Sid's colleagues *didn't understand his explanation of how the machine works.*

b Sid's colleagues *didn't understand when he explained how the machine works.*

Both sentence **a** and sentence **b** are correct as *his explanation* and *when he explained* carry the same information as the original sentence.

Look at these answers. Which ones are acceptable transformations?

1   Sid's colleagues *failed to understand his explanation of how the machine works.*

2   Sid's colleagues *failed to understand when he tried to explain how the machine works.*

3   Sid's colleagues *didn't understand when he tried to explain how the machine works.*

4   Sid's colleagues *understood nothing when he tried to explain how the machine works.*

5   Sid's colleagues *understood little of his explanation of how the machine works.*

4   For sentences **1–5** decide whether **a** and **b** are good or bad transformations.

1   It was once thought that the sun moved around the earth.

  a   The sun *used to move around the earth once.*
  b   The sun *was once thought to move around the earth.*

2   Everyone started clapping immediately the curtain came down.

  a   No sooner *had the curtain come down than everyone started clapping.*
  b   No sooner *had everyone started clapping when the curtain came down.*

3   He didn't intend to pay the phone bill until the last possible moment.

  a   He had *to pay the phone bill at the last possible moment.*
  b   He had *no intention of paying the phone bill until the last possible moment.*

4   Despite his bad headache, he still completed the exam successfully.

  a   Although *he had a bad headache, he still completed the exam successfully.*
  b   Although *he was suffering from a bad headache, he still completed the exam successfully.*

5   They were unable to open the door until they found a spare key.

  a   Not until *a spare key was found were they able to open the door.*
  b   Not until *a person was found with a spare key they were able to open the door.*

REMEMBER

- Check that the new sentence is similar in meaning to the original sentence.

- Try to identify the target structure of each transformation sentence.

- Do not make changes or additions which are not necessary.

- In the new sentence try to use words which have the same root as words in the original sentence.

5 Now try these exercises. Finish each of the following sentences in such a way that it is as similar as possible in meaning to the sentence printed before it.

1 One of the actors was too ill to appear in the play that night.
One actor was so _____
.

2 I am astounded that you paid the money before you received the goods.
What _____ .

3 The price of computers has fallen significantly in the last five years.
There has _____ .

4 Sarah finds it easy to learn foreign languages.
Sarah has no _____ .

5 She was appointed to the committee for two years.
Her _____ .

6 Tony agreed to appear in the play on condition that he didn't have to sing.
Tony said, 'As _____ '.

7 I will get in touch with you immediately Sue gives me an answer.
As _____ .

8 Over the years, unpainted woodwork tends to rot.
If _____ .

9 It's extremely important that Rachel avoids upsetting Roger.
On no account _____ .

10 It was once thought that the stars moved around the earth.
The stars _____ .

11 I'd prefer you not to smoke in the car, if you don't mind.
I'd rather _____ .

12 I'm sorry we're unable to invite Mark to the party.
I wish _____ .

1 In this section you must choose the word or phrase, **A**, **B**, **C** or **D** which best completes each sentence.

1 I'm afraid she's feeling very _____ up at the moment, due to stress at work.

    A coiled   **B** turned   **C** locked   **D** wound

2 Under extreme provocation, this type of person might _____ to violence.

    A revenge   **B** resume   **C** recourse   **D** resort

3 Cutting down trees allowed the Prime Minister to give _____ to his emotions.

    A vent   **B** wind   **C** duct   **D** flow

4 Scientists are on the _____ of proving the theory.

    A lip   **B** edge   **C** brink   **D** cusp

5 What happened astonished _____ who witnessed it.

    A such   **B** them   **C** ones   **D** those

6 No sooner _____ John arrived, than it started to rain.

    A when   **B** did   **C** had   **D** got

7 Whatever you may say, I still think honesty is the best _____ .

    A rule   **B** belief   **C** method   **D** policy

8 Far _____ being helpful, he often appeared quite rude.

    A away   **B** from   **C** than   **D** without

9 There is no scientific _____ to support his theory.

    A evidence   **B** indication   **C** testimony   **D** declaration

10 Mark and Paula were both very focused _____ their careers.

    A at   **B** on   **C** with   **D** in

2 Fill each of the numbered blanks in the passage with **one** suitable word.

I hate holidays

It's years now since anyone told me I needed a holiday. That is because I long (**1**) _____ ran out of companions who were prepared to put (**2**) _____ with a two-week sulk. The only way could cope (**3**) _____ a holiday was by taking my lap-top with me and working (**4**) _____ they poked among some ruins in the morning. I was reasonable company over lunch, (**5**) _____ in the afternoon, when they (**6**) _____ dragged me off to the beach with cries of, 'You're on holiday, for goodness sake!', I was intolerable.

Eventually, I came to (**7**) _____ with the fact that holidays (**8**) _____ I don't mix. Holidays, that is, (**9**) _____ the suntan lotion and beach towel variety. (**10**) _____, I reasoned, one reaches the end of a 'relaxing' holiday longing to get back to (**11**) _____ desk, what was the (**12**) _____ of setting off in the first place?

I do of course take breaks, but given my aversion (**13**) _____ both sand and grass, always in foreign cities. But there are strict ground rules. The (**14**) _____ is that my journey has to have some purpose. Maybe I'm writing a travel article, or catching (**15**) _____ with the local theatres. The reason can be pretty tenuous, but it has to be (**16**) _____ . Secondly, there are my requirements. The hotel has to have a fax machine and I must be able to tune (**17**) _____ the television news in my room. And (**18**) _____, I must be able to get the English newspapers, even if a few days late. With all (**19**) _____ factors in place, I am in (**20**) _____ element. But three days later, I'm ready to go home.

3 Fill each of the blanks with a suitable word or phrase.

1 Please don't exaggerate; I really feel you're making a _____ a molehill.

2 I'm afraid she was spoilt as a child; her parents always allowed her to _____ way.

3 It's really great! As a way of meeting new friends, going to the social club _____ beating.

4 The police promised to leave no _____ in their hunt for the murderer.

5 Please don't _____ bush, we need to get straight to the heart of the problem, if we are to solve it.

4 For each of the sentences below, write a new sentence as similar as possible in meaning to the original sentence, but using the word given. This word **must not be altered** in any way.

Example: A lot of people attended the meeting.

turnout

Answer: There was a very poor turnout for the meeting.

1 The couple walked along in complete silence; they could think of nothing to say to each other.

loss

_____

2 The other partner knew nothing about what was happening.

aware

_____

3 In all probability a disharmonious relationship will result from negative thoughts.

likely

_____

4 A lover's tiff is painful, even when it takes place in private.

doors

_____

5 Richard and Donna had ended their relationship three months earlier.

split

_____

6 I'm quite prepared to help out in an emergency.

mind

_____

7 A stamped addressed envelope should be enclosed with your order.

accompanied

_____

8 People shouldn't be allowed to smoke in public places.

prohibited

_____

9 The eye disease glaucoma is thought to affect around 2% of the population.

suffer

_____

10 I was asked if I would like a hamburger or a cheeseburger.

choice

_____

All Right on the Night

SPEAKING 1

Expressing likes and dislikes

1   Look at these video covers. What types of film are they?
Match each of the covers with a genre from the box.

thriller   science fiction   comedy   western
costume drama   horror   romance   cartoon

2 Discuss these questions with your partner.

Have you seen any of these films? What was it like?
Which of these genre do you particularly like or dislike? Why?
What are the conventions of the genre in each case?
Why are these types of film popular? Who do they appeal to?
What types of film are becoming more/less popular? Why is this?

3 Look at these three video covers. What do the films all have in common?

At what age should young people be allowed to see films like these?

  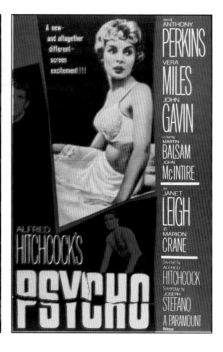

4 Talk to your partner. Do you agree with the following?

All modern Hollywood films look the same.

Explicit sex scenes in films are degrading to women.

Scenes of violence on film lead people to be more violent in real life.

Film censorship is an evil thing that seeks to stifle artistic expression

LISTENING 1
Multiple choice

You will hear a radio programme about violence in films. For questions **1–4** choose the answer **A**, **B**, **C** or **D** which you think fits best according to what you hear.

1   What does Dr Drew feel about the research that's been carried out?

  A There's too much of it.
  B It hasn't been well conducted.
  C It has been unsuccessful.
  D It has been inconclusive.

2   Dr Drew thinks that advertising

  A leads people to behave unpredictably.
  B affects people differently to movies.
  C sets out to alter people's tastes.
  D makes use of views people already hold.

3   What does the interviewer feel about explicit violence on film?

  A She likes advanced warning of it.
  B It never fails to shock her.
  C She's become hardened to it.
  D It holds no interest for her.

4   According to Dr Drew, what is the main problem with violent films?

  A They fail to use good imagery.
  B They don't have interesting plots.
  C They leave little to the imagination.
  D They are in bad taste.

PRONUNCIATION
Word stress

1   Look at these words from the listening. Underline the stressed syllable in each word.

  Example: ac<u>claim</u>ed

  reaffirmed   distasteful   inconclusive   unsuccessful   unpredictably
  Now listen to check.

2   Now draw lines on these words to show the boundaries between
  ● root words   ● prefixes   ● suffixes

  Example: ac|claim|ed

  What general rules can you identify about the stress in words like these?

3   Listen to these groups of words and underline the stressed syllable in each word.
  1   real   reality   realism   really   unreality
  2   photograph   photographic   photography   photographer
  3   family   familiar   unfamiliar   familiarity
  4   market   marketing   marketable   unmarketable
  5   person   personal   impersonal   personality   impersonation
  6   inform   informative   uninformative   information
  7   product   production   productive   unproductive
  8   manage   manager   management   mismanagement

Cloze passage

Read the text below and decide which word **A**, **B**, **C** or **D** best fits each blank. The first one has been done for you as an example.

Film posters

Film posters (**0**) ___*used*___ to be considered worthless ephemera once they'd (**1**) _____ their purpose – to get bums on (**2**) _____ . They took up too much space in warehouses and were destroyed (**3**) _____ the thousand. No one (**4**) _____ to lay them down on acid-free paper to (**5**) _____ them from discolouring or to guard (**6**) _____ pinholes and creases in (**7**) _____ of the day they could be sold for (**8**) _____ sums of money.

Today, more and more people are (**9**) _____ film posters as works of art. The art market is normally beyond people's (**10**) _____ , so they are looking for images they can afford. The market is partly (**11**) _____ by nostalgia. David Hutchinson is a typical collector with what he is (**12**) _____ to call an addiction. 'I loved film posters as a child and I've been (**13**) _____ ever since', he says.

People collect posters of well-known films, or ones they (**14**) _____ with some memory, like their first date. Sometimes, (**15**) _____ , a poster of an obscure 'twenties' film may have a fantastic image and that's what (**16**) _____ . Only posters with good graphics (**17**) _____ muster with serious collectors, however.

Today's posters are photographic and so (**18**) _____ the elements that collectors like – the design and artwork. They'll also never be as (**19**) _____ as older posters, as thousands are printed, so more of them are (**20**) _____ to survive.

0	**A** longed	**B** used	**C** ended	**D** wanted
1	**A** served	**B** performed	**C** satisfied	**D** delivered
2	**A** chairs	**B** seats	**C** stalls	**D** places
3	**A** in	**B** by	**C** at	**D** on
4	**A** remembered	**B** thought	**C** imagined	**D** wondered
5	**A** stop	**B** seal	**C** store	**D** hold
6	**A** around	**B** for	**C** from	**D** against
7	**A** prediction	**B** investment	**C** anticipation	**D** foresight

8	**A** inopportune	**B** exorbitant	**C** extreme	**D** inordinate
9	**A** eyeing	**B** seeing	**C** watching	**D** looking
10	**A** stretch	**B** reach	**C** hold	**D** touch
11	**A** driven	**B** pushed	**C** powered	**D** urged
12	**A** merry	**B** happy	**C** jolly	**D** funny
13	**A** hooked	**B** nailed	**C** stuck	**D** fixed
14	**A** accompany	**B** correlate	**C** associate	**D** affiliate
15	**A** regardless	**B** although	**C** moreover	**D** however
16	**A** counts	**B** reckons	**C** catches	**D** minds
17	**A** win	**B** take	**C** get	**D** pass
18	**A** want	**B** lack	**C** miss	**D** fail
19	**A** rewarding	**B** valuable	**C** profitable	**D** worthwhile
20	**A** ready	**B** likely	**C** prone	**D** willing

Sentence completion

1 Look at the picture of Marilyn Monroe.

Have you ever seen a Marilyn Monroe film?
What type of film do you associate with Marilyn Monroe?
What type of parts did she play?
Why is she such an important figure in film history?
What else do you know about her?

2 You will hear a radio discussion about Marilyn Monroe. For questions **1–14** complete the sentences with a word or short phrase.

Sue says the play doesn't require [___1___] of Marilyn.

Sue says the play shows us that Marilyn was really [___2___] .

David's story shows us that Marilyn could control the extent to which people [___3___] .

David points out that Marilyn couldn't really choose [___4___] .

Unlike other actresses, Marilyn [___5___] the stereotypical image.

In the 1950s, middle-class audiences regarded Marilyn as [___6___] .

Now people realize how much her image was created by [___7___] .

Sue admires Marilyn as both a [___8___] and [___9___] .

Sue says that the dress was difficult [___10___] .

Marilyn felt that the costumes for *The Seven Year Itch* were too [___11___] .

Sue is interested by the fact that Marilyn [___12___] the dress and that it was bought [___13___] .

David feels that the image of the dress is enhanced by the fact that Marilyn's [___14___] .

3 Discuss these questions with your partner.

How was the real Marilyn different from the image?
Do modern film stars have more control over their screen image?
Why do celebrities often seem to have unhappy private lives?

PHRASAL VERBS 1

1 Underline the phrasal verb in this sentence.

If you have a bad day at work you can't take it out on your family.

2 Complete each sentence with a suitable verb.

1 'I'd like to _____ you up on your offer of a lift' said John.

2 The concert was boring, the guitarist certainly didn't _____ up to his reputation.

3 Ray walks so fast it's difficult to _____ up with him.

4 The play was cancelled as most of the cast had _____ down with flu.

5 The local cinema has decided to _____ away with its advanced booking system.

6 The organizers of the pop festival admitted they'd _____ up against some technical problems.

GRAMMAR 1
'Whatever' clauses

1 Look at these sentences from the article.

Whatever the cynic might have to say about media-hype and 'marketability', there can be no disputing the sheer uniqueness of this musical phenomenon.

Whatever imperfections he elucidates, there are always compliments accompanying them …

What is the function of the word *whatever* in these sentences?

2 Rewrite these sentences with a phrase beginning with *Whatever*. What extra meaning is given by the addition of *may/might* to the sentences?

1 I don't care what you say, he's a brilliant singer.

Whatever _____

2 It doesn't matter what you think of her, you must admit she has a beautiful voice.

Whatever _____

3 He makes all kinds of mistakes, but he doesn't lose his concentration.

Whatever _____

4 I don't mind what you do, but don't forget to watch *La Traviata* on the TV tonight.

Whatever _____

5 You may say she has a difficult temperament, but her voice is lovely.

Whatever _____

6 She may choose to sing any kind of song but her voice is always perfect.

Whatever _____

📖 N.B. The Workbook has further exercises of this type.

Comprehension

1 Read this article and answer the questions which follow it.

Opera's Wedding of the Century

OF ALL SINGING marriages this must be the most spectacularly operatic ever. Love, tragedy and triumph abound in the story of Roberto Alagna and Angela Gheorghiu. Only a year ago Alagna was being hailed the new Pavarotti after a couple of performances of 'La Boheme' and 'Romeo and Juliet'.
10 *Meanwhile Gheorghiu's 'Traviata' had catapulted her to overnight stardom at 29.*

It was certainly good for business when they announced their love for each other last May. But so soon after the early death of Alagna's first wife, expectations were not high. They are now married. Both are musical sensations in their own right and I
20 met them in a London recording studio singing love songs for a new disc. Whatever the cynic might have to say about media-hype and 'marketability', there can be no disputing the sheer uniqueness of this musical phenomenon.

Roberto Alagna is a small man who tends to remain relatively still while singing. But his stance, with feet
30 spread squarely apart, arms out at his sides like a fighter entering a fray, back arched and head tilted slightly upwards, lends him a tremendously imposing presence. When the most strenuous and demanding high note falters and is to be consigned to digital limbo, or a song goes sadly awry for the fourth time, his face never fails to light up in amusement.

40 In contrast, Gheorghiu with fluid movement of arms and hands, conducts the passage of her voice as if coaxing it, manipulating it. She fidgets, looking like she's unable to find the most comfortable way to stand. When mistakes are made she might clasp herself in exasperation or feign banging her head against the music stand, but this is not serious
50 vexation – more the humorous antics of an extrovert perfectionist striving to produce the results she knows she's capable of. They often end with her bursting into fits of giggles.

Throughout the session producer David Groves exhibits total composure and control, in spite of the frenetic rate of communication with the conductor and the arduous nature of
60 eliciting the very best from the singers. Whatever imperfections he

elucidates, there are always compliments accompanying them, and his patience seems limitless. After an hour of tussling with a particularly tricky piece his message to the conductor is 'I think Roberto is a fraction behind Angela, but the phrasing is perfect.' Then, turning aside to those gathered around him and without a hint of
70 irritation: 'It would be so wonderful if they could just end up in the same place at the same time!'

Then he is suddenly satisfied, announcing: 'Boheme, please, Boheme.' After the travails of the previous hour, the relief at the prospect of singing from this opera is palpable. It's the work that brought them together and 'O Soave Fancuilla' obviously touches on something special. The soloists
80 share a plane apart, their pointing fingers, furrowed brows and bubbling laughter culminating in an embrace that bridges the two-foot gulf between them. And unbelievably, there's not a camera in sight.

1 What does the phrase 'catapulted her to overnight stardom' in lines 11–12 tell us about Angela Gheorgiu's career?

2 Why is the writer surprised that the couple are now married?

3 Why might some people be cynical about the new disc?

4 What does the writer mean by 'entering a fray'? (line 31)

5 What does the phrase 'consigned to digital limbo' in lines 36–37 imply?

6 What do you understand by the word 'fidgets'? (line 44)

7 In your own words, compare the reactions of Roberto and Angela to mistakes they make?

8 Which three words in paragraph five are used to underline the difficulties of David Groves' work?

9 Which phrase in paragraph five provides an example of David Groves' great patience?

10 What does 'palpable' in line 77 mean?

11 In your own words, describe the writer's feelings about the performance of *O Soave Fancuilla* which he has heard?

12 What is it that the writer finds so surprising at the end of the piece?

2 Find words or phrases in the article that mean (paragraph numbers in brackets):

a publicity (2)

b way of standing (3)

c trying hard (4)

d hold tightly (4)

e pretend (4)

f gently encouraging (4)

g uncontrollable laughter (4)

Reported speech

1 Look at these two sentences from the article. Both are in direct speech.

'I think Roberto is a fraction behind Angela, but the phrasing is perfect.' (said David)

'It would be so wonderful if they could just end up in the same place at the same time!' (said David)

2 Rewrite the sentences in reported speech.

David said

_____

David said

_____

3 Which two general rules of reported speech do these examples illustrate?

4 What other types of changes are necessary in reported speech?

📖 N. B. The Workbook has further work on reported speech.

ANGELA GHEORGHIU: The Inside Story

Discovered: Bucharest Music Academy 1990

Big break: Violetta in *La Traviata* receives such outstanding reviews that TV channels immediately clear their schedules for immediate transmission. The CD wins 'Disc of the Year'.

What the critics say: 'She is the most affecting Violetta for decades'.'Will she be spoilt by instant success?' 'She's stable, focused, extremely choosy.' 'I just hope this early success doesn't go to her head and take out the spontaneity and emotion.'

What she says about herself: 'There was never any question of 'Oh, what a promising voice!' I was born with this voice. Right from when I was a little girl, it was clear that I would become a singer.'

What she says about Alagna: 'We work together, in the same room; we are quick learners. We talk about music for hours. We are in love with this profession. We are one with each other, we try to help each other be our best. We have so much in common.'

WRITING 1
Describing people

1 Work with a partner. One of you read the *Inside Story* notes about Angela and the other read about Roberto.

2 Tell your partner what new information you have found. Use the headings in the text to ask and answer questions about Roberto and Angela.

3 Use the information you have found, plus anything else from the article on pages 88 and 89 to write a short article comparing the careers of the famous couple. Use your own words as far as possible.

Use these headings for your paragraphs:

- Early careers
- What the critics think of them
- What they say about themselves
- Working together – the future

ROBERTO ALAGNA: The Inside Story

Discovered: In a Paris pizzeria, where he sang eight hours a night for tips.

Main roles: *La Traviata* at *La Scala*, Milan in 1993; Romeo in London in 1994

What the critics say: 'Will he be spoilt by instant success?' 'Is he just another example of our hunger for the instant star?'

What he says about himself: 'Like any other singer I want my own identity. I wonder if I please people because I'm like another singer or because I'm me. There's nothing calculated in my interpretation. I sing what I feel. My style isn't new, it's just mine.'

What he says about Gheorghiu: 'We'd like to build a career together. We don't accept offers to sing together for the sake of it. With our rapport we could do great things. Angela is more prudent than me. I'm a bit exuberant. I have to do everything at once. She's calmer; she has serenity.'

HELP WITH TALKING ABOUT A PASSAGE

The second part of Paper 5 requires you to speak about a short passage. This will be linked in some way to the picture(s) you have spoken about in Part One.

■**1** There are some important points to remember about this part of the test.

1 You will be given time to read the passage, but you do not have to read it aloud.

2 This is not a test of reading comprehension, so there is no need to worry if you do not understand some of the words or ideas expressed.

3 The examiner/your partner has also read the passage and knows what it contains. Don't just repeat the main points of information, but talk about the language used and ideas expressed with the examiners/your partner.

4 You are generally asked to think about where the passage might be found. Be ready to give an opinion with some reasons to back this up.

■**2** Many students find talking about the passage difficult. Here is a list of ideas to help you talk about a passage. Ask yourself the following questions:

A Where does it come from?

1 Is the passage from a written text or is it someone speaking? Find some examples of words and phrases to back up your ideas.

2 Where would you see/hear this sort of passage? For example:
   - in a newspaper
   - in a textbook
   - in a novel
   - on the radio/TV

Say why you think so.

3 What is the style of the passage?

Is the passage: formal
                 informal
                 neutral
                 impersonal, etc.
                 conversational
                 literary
                 technical
                 academic, etc.

Is the style: journalistic
               colloquial
               literary
               descriptive?

Is it written/spoken in the: first person
                              second person
                              third person
                              passive, etc.?

Give examples of actual words and phrases to support your opinions.

4 What is the function of the passage? For example:

giving information   entertaining   advising   warning
instructing   persuading

5 Who is the passage meant for?

Who is meant to read/hear it?   the general public   students
                                a friend   colleagues, etc.

B What do you think about the passage?

Do you like it?
Do you agree with the ideas expressed?
Does it remind you of other situations/examples?

Be prepared to expand the topic. Remember that this part of the interview only lasts two or three minutes including the time it takes to read the passage. You will be discussing these points with the examiner or your partner(s) so you don't have to speak all that time.

Practise talking to your partner about passages 2 and 3. Work through the points in **A** and **B** for each passage, finding as many things to say as possible.

Passage 1

For thousands of years, pigs have been an important part of farming life. But these days, it is not just the farmers who respect their worth. More and more people are gaining an appreciation of the individual charm and intelligence of these animals.

The Perfect Pigs Collection is sure to delight collectors with the remarkable authenticity modeller Martyn Alcock has achieved. He has used sculptor's resin in order to capture the tiniest of details with great accuracy. On closer inspection, you will see the unique characteristics of each pig are brought to life in perfect detail.

Passage 2

Getting to the church on time is fundamental. When approaching a car hire company for the big day you should check that a quote includes any extras and a clear breakdown of how the transport is arranged and, of course, the type of vehicles.

A vintage choice may be ideal for town or short journeys but not country lanes between villages. Similarly, people often ask for cabriolet-type vehicles which have limited leg room in the rear. So, your best bet is a modern Rolls-Royces with air conditioning, plenty of leg room, lambswool rugs and even footstools. What more could you want?

Passage 3

The bakery is open every day. I go to bed at around 2 pm and get up at 10 pm.

I live in Peckham and cycle to work at 12.30 am. We get a few dodgy customers; some don't want to or can't pay; others are off their heads and buy loads of bagels; and you get people from night-clubs. One of the papers said we had a riot a few years ago, but it was more a fight between two guys. One woman sat on the counter with her stiletto heels in the cream cakes. Working here has made me tough. If you get grief from one customer, you can't take it out on the next.

⬚ LISTENING 3

Matching

1 You will hear two reviewers, John and Lynn, talking about a book they've both been reading. For questions **1–8**, decide whose opinion is being reported. Write **J** for John, **L** for Lynn or **B** for both of them.

1 The plot is inadequate.   1 ⬚

2 The situation described is not very original.   2 ⬚

3 It's difficult to relate to the characters.   3 ⬚

4 The subject matter is thought provoking.   4 ⬚

5 The book is well-suited to a film version.   5 ⬚

6 The film raises important issues.   6 ⬚

7 The book is quite frightening in parts.   7 ⬚

8 Generally my opinion of the book is favourable.   8 ⬚

2 Listen again and find expressions that mean:

1 to be precise (Lynn)
2 in my opinion (Lynn)
3 Really? You must be joking! (Lynn)
4 it's a normal situation (John)
5 there are many of them (Lynn)
6 with lots of noise and action (Lynn)
7 very involved and excited (Lynn)
8 a very readable book (John)

READING 2

Reading for main points and specific information

1 Look at these reviews of various events. Read them quickly and decide which branch of the arts each review is dealing with.

2 Now read again more carefully and decide if each passage gives a positive or negative review of the performance or product. Underline the words or phrases which indicate the writer's opinion.

3 Match each of these statements **1–8** with one of the passages **A–F**.

1 It was better than I expected. ___   ___

2 It is becoming increasingly popular. ___

3 It is an adaptation from another medium. ___

4 You can never be sure what you'll see. ___

5 It's an opportunity to see some masterpieces. ___

6 It is less explicit than some works. ___

7 One performance stands out. ___

8 It is faithful to the original artist's ideas. ___

Perlman Joins the Party

There can be few more unpleasant musical experiences than listening to someone whose performances you have respected make a fool of themselves with unfamiliar repertoire. The classical disc catalogue is littered with embarrassing examples of this particular folly. Thankfully, on his latest release, Perlman has collaborated with some of the best exponents of the form – the excellent *Klezmatics* who add a modern jazz approach and the more traditional *Brave New World*, redolent of paprika and strong coffee. Perlman is totally within style, part of the band, part of the party, not the star turn.

B

STREET FIGHTER

Like many before him, director de Souza falls foul of transferring a necessarily repetitive computer game to the big screen: instead of a fluid cinematic narrative, we have a stop-start plot with too many heroes, multiple plot threads, and virtually no suspense or excitement. Having taken hostage 63 aid workers and a handful of Allied Forces soldiers renegade warlord General M Bison (Raul Julia) demands a hefty ransom. Colonel Guile (Jean-Claude van Damme) and more than a dozen multi-ethnic heroes then try to penetrate the defences of Bison's hi-tech fortress. The late Julia hams it up shamelessly as the camp commandant, but not even his suave presence and throw-away quips can save this noisy, brainless mess.

C

MORE TALES FROM THE ATTIC

If you love horror stories but blanch at sex and violence, Diana Guest's new work, *Forbidden Garden* could be what you've been waiting for. One night, journalist Patrick Kaiser hears the sound of sobbing coming from the end of his garden. Going outside to investigate, he swiftly becomes involved with a family whose two children, Hildy and Christian, live in mortal terror of their monstrous father, the celebrated pianist Julian Ferrare. What unnatural hold does this man have over his family? And what binds Hildy and Christian so tightly to the attic at the top of the house? Kaiser's attempts to discover the secrets of this mysterious foursome and his fight to protect the children from the evil around them lead us into a nightmarish world that simply can't fail to grip and compel. Read it if you dare.

D

Fortnight Club

The latest in a series of fascinating fortnightly shows where a large bunch of experienced comics try out new material and play around with new ideas in a friendly and relaxed atmosphere. Go for the surprises, go for the fun, but don't expect performers to trot out their regular acts. Above all – go early, as word is getting round! The quality can't be guaranteed but it makes for a fascinating night out.

E

BRUCE CRASTLEY

CRASTLEY'S REPUTATION as a master of light and shadow is certainly borne out in this generous twenty-year retrospective. Most of the quiet, warm-toned views here – of fireworks over the Brooklyn Bridge, sculpture fragments at the Met, a window of the Louvre – are impeccably balanced, meditative studies. But *For Lisette* (1976) and *Waiting Grand Central* (1983), push further into the poetic and daring, fragile compositions and a wealth of black tones that produce complex, nearly flawless gems. Through March 23.

F

──── THE RIVALS ────

R B Sheridan's sparkling eighteenth century comedy of moneyed manners **The Rivals** is a production which could have been showy, flouncy and self-satisfying beyond endurance. But it's actually quite a hoot, not least because, as well as carrying off the play's formidable wit, most of the performers manage to reflect Sheridan's redeeming undercurrent of generosity, even towards his most absurdly affected characters. This is the kind of show that might well give frothy costume comedies a good name.

VOCABULARY 1
Using your dictionary

■1 Look up these words from the reviews in your dictionary. Which meaning of the word is used here? What other meanings are there?

1	turn (A)	**4**	celebrated (C)	**7**	gems (E)
2	fluid (B)	**5**	bunch (D)	**8**	hoot (F)
3	threads (B)	**6**	quiet (E)	**9**	frothy (F)

WRITING 2
Reviews

■1 Which tense is used most of the time in each of the reviews? Underline instances where other tenses have been used. Why have they been used in each case?

■2 You have been asked to write a review for a magazine.

1 Choose a film, play or book which you have seen or read recently.

2 Think about:

- Who will read your review?
- What does your reader want to know?
- Why will your reader want to read your review?
- How much of the plot do you want a review to tell you?

3 Look back at the film, play and book reviews on pages 94 and 95.

Do they tell you what you want to know about the event?
How is the information organized in each of them?
In each case, comment on the style of the writing.
Which style do you prefer? Why?

4 Decide which of the following points you want to include in your review.

> genre   plot   characters   style of director/writer   performances
> costumes   ideas   who will like it   visuals   my opinion of it

Then divide the points into paragraphs depending on how you want to present the information.

5 Decide on the style you want to use. For example serious, journalistic, light-hearted, sarcastic, objective, etc. This should reflect your readership.

6 Now write your review. The words and expressions in the box may help you.

> it deals with ...
> it is set in ...
> the plot revolves around/focuses on ...
> it is produced/directed by ...
> I was particularly impressed/disappointed by ...
> it stars ...
> it will appeal to lovers/fans of ...
> it tells the story of ...
> it conveys a sense of ...

1 In this section you must choose the word or phrase, **A**, **B**, **C** or **D**, which best completes each sentence.

1 Many of the most _____ acclaimed films are also the most violent.

   A widely   **B** deeply   **C** broadly   **D** amply

2 I think it would be wrong to _____ to conclusions before we hear the details.

   A bounce   **B** hop   **C** skip   **D** jump

3 His memory was _____ by something he saw in a newspaper.

   A nudged   **B** jolted   **C** jogged   **D** prodded

4 When nervous, she has been known to burst into a _____ of the giggles.

   A turn   **B** fit   **C** spell   **D** bout

5 Some movies _____ on the fear that people have of being alone in old houses.

   A dwell   **B** abide   **C** lodge   **D** reside

6 If Richard feels he's been insulted he's _____ to get violent.

   A liable   **B** vulnerable   **C** prone   **D** subject

7 A lot of research has gone into looking for a _____ between films and behaviour.

   A link   **B** join   **C** chain   **D** thread

8 Sue found playing the difficult part of Marilyn Monroe on stage a _____ order.

   A big   **B** high   **C** great   **D** tall

9 After the concert, Roberto was being _____ as the new Pavarotti.

   A called   **B** cited   **C** hailed   **D** spoken

10 When he makes a mistake, the singer's face _____ up with amusement.

   A glows   **B** lights   **C** shines   **D** grins

2 Fill each of the numbered blanks in the passage with **one** suitable word.

Does music make you sharp?

For centuries people have believed that music can have lasting effects on our development. Jeanne d'Albret, the mother of the French king Henry IV, reportedly (**1**) _____ music played her every morning while she was pregnant (**2**) _____ the belief that it would mould the character of her unborn child and (**3**) _____ him having 'dark' moods. Historians have since (**4**) _____ Henry as jovial, but this anecdotal evidence is (**5**) _____ to convince sceptics that music can really beneficially affect development.

Recently a range of cognitive, emotional, motivational and social skills has (**6**) _____ claimed to benefit (**7**) _____ children's involvement with music. But conclusive (**8**) _____ is hard to find because it is difficult to isolate musical influences from many others that might (**9**) _____ a difference.

Research reported by Frances Rauscher in California, however, has claimed that listening to Mozart for ten minutes directly affects spatial reasoning skills. She suggested that students did (**10**) _____ after listening to the music because Mozart's writing is 'cognitively complex' and stimulates particular activity in the right half of the brain, (**11**) _____ then influences spatial reasoning in structures (**12**) _____ nearby. She argues that if children are (**13**) _____ to complex music from an early age, their spatial reasoning will improve. (**14**) _____ listening simple repetitive music, (**15**) _____ as rock music will impair performance.

Scientists will remain sceptical (**16**) _____ this small study is replicated, and this has proved difficult. One possible interpretation suggests that improvements in spatial reasoning occurred because music affects arousal, emotion (**17**) _____ both. Recent research undertaken at the Institute of Education has shown that (**18**) _____ quiet, relaxing, but cheerful, music to children (**19**) _____ are experiencing emotional and behavioural difficulties while they (**20**) _____ on mathematics problems, improves their behaviour and their test scores.

3 Fill each of the blanks with a suitable word or phrase.

1 The painting looks nice at a distance, but _____ inspection, it's not so good.

2 The film was really gripping; I was _____ my seat the whole time.

3 It looks like a designer dress, but actually she bought it _____ peg.

4 Whatever distractions there were around him, the actor never once seemed _____ concentration.

5 In attempting to play that unsuitable piece of music, the violinist risked _____ fool of himself.

4 For each of the sentences below, write a new sentence as similar as possible in meaning to the original sentence, but using the word given. This word **must not be altered** in any way.

Example: A lot of people attended the meeting.
>   **turnout**
Answer: *There was a very good turnout for the meeting.*

1 Although they believe it's not the case, most people are actually rather sentimental about animals.

contrary

_____

2 If you don't like this type of cake, you can try another.

liking

_____

3 In my opinion, the best tea is made in a teapot.

mind

_____

4 I was told either to accept the chairperson's decision or leave the society.

option

_____

5 Our teacher mentioned in passing that you can knit with dog hair.

happened

_____

6 I don't feel much like going to see that film tonight after all.

mood

_____

7 I doubt if the outdoor concert will go ahead in this weather.

hardly

_____

8 It was Amanda who pointed out Robin's beautiful voice to the director.

drew

_____

9 I didn't open the gate for fear of the dog attacking me.

frightened

_____

10 The thought of having a tooth extracted terrifies me.

hair

_____

5 Finish each of the following sentences in such a way that it is as similar as possible in meaning to the sentence printed before it.

Example: Immediately after his departure, things improved.

Answer: No sooner *had he departed than things improved.*

1 I only went to visit the art exhibition because my brother recommended it.

Had it not _____ .

2 Major rock bands have rarely visited this town.

There have _____ .

3 As I see more abstract paintings, I like them less and less.

The more _____ .

4 While I really do not like ballet, I'm prepared to go with you this time.

Despite my _____ .

5 The box office manager told me that the performance would finish at about ten-thirty tomorrow.

According _____ .

6 Steve hasn't had his hair cut for over six months.

It is _____ .

7 Even a full concert hall this evening will not mean that we cover our costs.

No matter _____ .

8 I enjoy listening to the radio much more than watching television.

I much _____ .

9 It is highly unlikely that the play will finish before 11 o'clock.

There _____ .

10 Whenever I go into that music shop, I spend more than I intend to.

I can't go _____ .

Tip of my Tongue

Talking about photographs

1 Look at the two photographs. Make a list of the similarities and differences between them. Think about:

The setting:
   where it is
   why it's happening

The people:
   their appearance
   their relationship with one another
   their feelings

The subject:
   how the photograph has been taken
   why the photograph has been taken
   where/how the photograph might be used

2 Talk to your partner about the photographs. Use the language in the box to compare and contrast them.

> they are both
> they both show
> both of them
> whereas
> on the other hand
> while
> it makes me think of
> I think they must/can't/could/may/
> might be...

3 What is the relationship between people, memory and computers? Think for a few minutes and make some notes or draw a mind map.

4 Discuss your ideas with your partner, agreeing and disagreeing as appropriate.

LISTENING 1

Part One

Listening for specific information

1 Talk to your partner about the Internet. Discuss these points:

- what experience you have of it
- your understanding of how it works
- how important you think it is
- the implications for English and other languages

2 You will hear the beginning of a radio programme about the language used on the Internet. As you listen, choose the two main points Bob Elman makes.

A The Internet should use a variety of languages.

B The English used on the Internet is nothing like everyday English.

C Human interaction would be easier if everyone spoke the same language.

D The jargon used on the Internet will soon develop into a whole new language which English speakers won't be able to understand.

E It's inevitable that languages change to meet new conditions.

3 Before you listen to the rest of the programme, make a list of words and expressions which are commonly used in relation to the Internet.

4 Listen to a continuation of the programme. How many of the words on your list are used by the speakers?

Part Two

Note taking

Listen to the rest of the radio programme again and complete the table on page 103.

VOCABULARY 1

Record keeping

1 Read this list of ways of organizing a vocabulary book. Discuss the advantages and drawbacks of each method with your partner.

a Chronological - like a diary, organized according to when you first came across them.

b Alphabetical - like a dictionary with words listed according to the letter they begin with.

c Under topic headings - e.g. sport, crime, Internet, etc.

d Grammatically - according to the type of word. e.g. verbs, nouns, etc.

e Another way?

2 Which of the following do you think it might also be useful to record?

- Examples of how the word was used e.g. ' to post a contribution'.
- References of where you heard/saw it so that you can look at the context again.
- The prepositions that are used with the word. e.g. 'in the context *of*'.
- The appropriate register/situation in which to use the word.
- How the word is pronounced and stressed.

3 When you have organized your vocabulary records, what is the best way to memorize the words it contains?

INTERNET LANGUAGE

Familiar words with a new meaning in the context of the Internet.

Word	Part of speech	Literal meaning	Meaning in this context
_____	verb	watersport	moving around net - you don't know where you're going
_____	verb	make a noise	making choices on the net by pressing a button
_____	noun	place/location of something	one user's contribution to the net
_____	verb	to send something	to put some material on the net
_____	noun	novice/newcomer	new user of net
_____	verb	exist unobserved	surfing without contributing to the net
_____	verb	to burn	to tell off

Examples of greetings and salutations:

_____ = abbreviation of _____

_____ = abbreviation of _____

Computer terms that are entering the common language:

_____ = still used though it no longer describes the object.

_____ = a noun that is now widely used as a verb.

_____ = has a wider range of meanings than the equivalent common words.

_____ = new meanings of this word seem likely to be used more widely.

Cloze passage

1 Before you complete the cloze passage answer these questions.

1 What are usually recognized as the five senses?

2 What type of things often get referred to as 'sixth sense'?

3 Have you ever had any experiences of this type?

4 Look at the words in the box. What does each one mean? In what context is each word generally used? Use your dictionary to help you if necessary.

surveillance	orthodox	phenomenon
ambush	telescopic	ludicrous

2 Fill each of the numbered blanks in the passage with **one** suitable word from the box below. The first one has been done for you as an example.

by	no	in	only	on	as	out
get	means	are	when	who	being	taking
to	have	at	far	around	not	which

Sixth sense

The idea that some people can sense when they are being stared (**0**) __at__ has so (**1**) _____ been rejected as ludicrous (**2**) _____ orthodox scientists. But now researchers in England and America are (**3**) _____ the claims more seriously.

According (**4**) _____ Cambridge University biologist Dr Rupert Sheldrake, the phenomenon has long been recognized (**5**) _____ fields such as wildlife photography and military surveillance. The security manager of a large store in London, for example, has caught thousands of people (**6**) _____ his surveillance cameras, and he is in (**7**) _____ doubt that some people have a 'sixth sense' of (**8**) _____ they are being watched. They can (**9**) _____ their backs to the camera, which may also be hidden, yet still (**10**) _____ agitated when the camera is trained on them. Some move on, whilst others look (**11**) _____ to try and spot the camera.

Some police teams (**12**) _____ said to have a rule about (**13**) _____ keeping people in telescopic sights too long because suspects may sense they are being watched. And the experience of a soldier (**14**) _____ had a strong sense of being watched as he patrolled along a dark alley one night (**15**) _____ to find later that he had narrowly missed (**16**) _____ ambushed is by no (**17**) _____ an uncommon one.

Dr Sheldrake is now gathering data on the staring phenomenon (**18**) _____ part of a scientific study and will be carrying (**19**) _____ experiments designed to measure staring sensitivity by monitoring skin resistance, (**20**) _____ he hopes will throw further light on the question.

VOCABULARY 2

Prefixes

1 What does the prefix *re* in front of a word often indicate?

2 Match each of the words in the box with one of the definitions **A–I**.

Note: two of the words have the same definition.

retrieve	repeat	recall	retain	record
remember	recognize	revise	remind	research

A Bring back into the memory   _____

B Identify/acknowledge   _____

C Set down in permanent form for reference   _____

D Say or do over again   _____

E Make or help someone remember something   _____

F To collect facts by scientific study   _____

G Succeed in not losing or forgetting   _____

H Find given information again in the memory   _____

I Read or look at again to improve familiarity   _____

3 Complete each sentence with a noun form of one of the verbs in the box. Use each verb only once, then mark the stressed syllable of the noun.

1 The _____ of numbers can help you to commit them to memory.

2 They made a _____ of the interview so that it could be broadcast later.

3 He was sent a _____ because he hadn't returned a library book.

4 She is working as a _____ at the local university.

5 He started a programme of _____ four weeks before the exam.

6 He said, 'Hello again', but there was no look of _____ in her eyes.

7 Long-term _____ of information requires more work than short-term.

8 Giving the first letter of a word speeded up its _____ from memory.

9 The statue was erected in _____ of the country's greatest writer.

10 I had no _____ of the events he described.

SPEAKING 2
Talking about personal abilities

1 Do you have a good memory? Are you better at remembering some things than others? Talk to your partner about the words in the box.

> numbers
> names
> lists of points
> appointments
> messages
> jokes
> songs/poems/quotations
> English vocabulary

A

2 Do you know any good methods for memorizing things?

3 Choose one of the two pictures labelled **A** or **B**. Look at your picture for one
minute then close the book. Tell your partner as many things about the
picture as you can remember. Your partner can look at the picture to check.
Change roles and repeat for the other picture.

B

Reading for specific information

1 How important is memory in learning a language? Does this affect your approach to studying English?

2 Read part one of an extract from a book about learning and memory and decide if the statements **1–6** are true or false.

1 Most people find it hard to keep unfamiliar telephone numbers in their head.

2 Most people need to keep repeating a new telephone number every thirty seconds in order to remember it.

3 Most people forget new telephone numbers if they do not actively try to remember them.

4 In the short term, it is difficult to remember more than seven new numbers or pieces of information at one time.

5 Long-term memory is also limited in terms of the number of items which can be remembered.

6 It is more difficult to commit information to long-term memory.

TYPES OF MEMORY: PART ONE

Most readers will be familiar with the experience of looking up a telephone number and then repeating it to themselves for the time it takes to sit down and dial the number. As luck would have it, this is invariably the occasion for someone to ask a distracting question with the result that the number is forgotten and has to be looked up all over again. Equally familiar and irritating is when you need the same number twenty-four hours later and find that you are quite unable to remember it.

These experiences reflect the widely recognized view among psychologists that with verbal learning the ability to hold information for brief periods (usually up to 30 seconds
10 in duration) demands fairly constant repetition, and any distraction or interruption is likely to severely impede that ability. Moreover, it has been established that our capacity for short-term retention is remarkably consistent, and that most people experience some breakdown in retention as soon as the number of items or chunks of information exceeds seven.

This type of memory, known as 'short-term memory', is clearly different from 'long-term memory', which is our capacity for recall of information minutes, weeks and years after the original input. Furthermore, the difference is not simply one of duration. Unlike short-term memory which is limited in capacity, long-term memory is seemingly inexhaustible and can accommodate any amount of new information. Not surprisingly,
20 this new information can be stored at a price; it is generally acknowledged that we need to work much harder to commit information to long-term memory, and the type of repetition we described as being essential to short term retention may not be adequate for long term retention.

3 Try this experiment in groups of three. Read **all** the instructions before you begin.

Decide who is Student A, Student B and Student C.
Spend 30 seconds trying to memorize a telephone number.
Then close the book and follow *your* instructions.

Student A:
Keep repeating the number in your mind.

Student B:
Think about what you had for dinner yesterday.

Student C:
Count to 20 out loud. First in your own language and
then in English.

When Student C has reached 20 in English, each try to write down the
telephone number.

The telephone number to remember is: 0136-227-8359615

Check with your partners to see how well each of you has remembered the number.

4 Discuss these terms and expressions with your partner. What do you think each one means?

a short-term memory   d low-frequency vocabulary
b long-term memory   e on the tip of my tongue
c the mental lexicon

5 Read another extract from the same book and decide if the statements **1–7** are true or false.

1 The speed at which we can recognize and recall words suggests that the 'mental lexicon' is very organized. ☐

2 It is likely that there are similarities between the organization of our 'mental lexicon' and the arrangement of a dictionary. ☐

3 In the Brown and McNeil experiment, some people could describe a sextant, but couldn't remember the name for it. ☐

4 In the Freedman and Loftus experiment, the results show that the second question was more difficult to understand than the first one. ☐

5 Words which are connected in meaning can be remembered together more easily. ☐

6 Words used often are more easily remembered than words used recently. ☐

7 Knowing about memory is important for language learners because of the limited time which they have for study. ☐

TYPES OF MEMORY: PART TWO

Which is the odd one out?

Our 'mental lexicon' is highly organized and efficient. Were storage of information haphazard, we would be forced to search in a random fashion to retrieve words; this simply is not feasible when one considers the speed at which we need to recognize and recall. Furthermore, it is extremely improbable that we organize words in the brain as a dictionary does. Imagine you 10 were trying to recall the word 'nozzle' for instance. It is unlikely that you would retrieve the word 'noxious' (which appears next to 'nozzle' in the dictionary) in place of the target word.

Some very interesting experiments carried out by Brown and McNeil exemplify this point forcefully and gives us clues about lexical organization. The experimenters gave testees definitions of low frequency vocabulary items and asked them to 20 name the item. One definition was 'A navigational instrument used in measuring angular distances, especially the altitude of the sun, moon and stars at sea'. Some testees were able to supply the correct answer (which was 'sextant'), but the researchers were more interested in the testees who had the answer 'on the tip of their tongues'. Some gave the answer 'compass', which seemed to indicate that they had accessed the right semantic field but found the wrong item. Others had a very 30 clear idea of the 'shape' of the item, and were often able to say how many syllables it had, what the first letter was, etc. It seems, then, that these systems are interrelated; at a very basic level there appears to be a phonological system, a system of meaning relations and a spelling system.

One way in which researchers investigate how the mental lexicon is organized is by comparing the speed at which people are able to recall items. It is generally accepted that if certain types of prompts 40 can be answered more quickly than others, then this will reflect the lexical system. Freedman and Loftus asked testees to perform two different types of tasks: e.g.
1 Name a fruit that begins with a 'p'.
2 Name a word beginning with a 'p' that is a fruit.

Testees were able to answer the first type of question more quickly than the second. This seems to indicate that 'fruits beginning with p' are categorized under 'fruit' rather than under a 50 'words beginning with p' heading. Furthermore, experimenters discovered in subsequent tests that once testees had access to the 'fruit' category, they were able to find other fruits more quickly. This seems to provide further evidence that semantically related items are 'stored together'. Most researchers appear to agree that items are arranged in a series of associative networks.

We also have to consider other variables which affect storage. One important factor here is 'word 60 frequency'; items which occur most frequently are also easily recognized and retrieved. Imagine a pile of cards, each representing an item of vocabulary. In this system the most frequently used words are 'at the top of the pile', and therefore easier to retrieve. 'Recency of use' is another variable, and, to return to the analogy of the pile, one can imagine words most recently used being at the top. These variables are concerned with the use of items, but it is also 70 important to consider when items were first learnt. Imagine a pile of words organized chronologically: the words learnt on the first day of a language course would be at one extreme and those most recently learnt at the other.

Clearly, native speakers do not acquire all their vocabulary in lexical sets, but rather acquire items in a haphazard, chronological fashion, generally in a fairly predictable order of frequency. However, native speakers have many years in 80 which to build up a comprehensive lexicon, whereas foreign learners are limited in this respect. Exploiting our present knowledge of storage systems to the full should allow us to attempt to speed up the learning process and facilitate storage.

WRITING 1
Summary

1 Look back at the second part of the extract and complete this summary of one of the experiments.

BROWN AND McNAIR'S EXPERIMENT

People were given _____ of low-frequency words and asked to say the word. Some

people gave the name of an object used in a similar situation to the one described. This proved

that their mental lexicon was divided into _____ .

Other people, who couldn't remember the word, could give the number of _____ or the

_____ . This proved that the mental lexicon is also organized according to

_____ and _____ .

---

2 Now write a similar summary of the second experiment, saying:

- what people had to do
- what results there were
- what the experiment proved

FREEDMAN AND LOFTUS' EXPERIMENT

Now discuss questions **3–5** with your partner.

3 Why are the following factors important for language students when they are trying to learn new words?

- how often words are used
- how recently the words were used
- when the words were learnt.

How can the pile of cards analogy help?

4 What do you understand about:

- the mental lexicon?
- semantic fields?

5 How will what you have read influence how you study and how you keep vocabulary records?

Conditionals

1 Look at this sentence from the passage.

Were storage of information to be haphazard, we would be forced to search in a random fashion to retrieve words.

1 What type of sentence is this?

2 What is the usual sequence of tenses in this type of sentence?

How is the example sentence different to this?

3 What other words can be used to begin this type of sentence?

4 Rewrite the example sentence so that the meaning is the same, but begin with the word *if*.

If _____

2 Finish each of the sentences **1–5** in such a way that it is as similar as possible in meaning to the sentence printed before it.

1 If you were more systematic in your approach, you would remember new words more easily.

Were _____

2 If you wrote that number down, you wouldn't keep forgetting it.

Were _____

3 If he listened to my advice, he wouldn't keep getting into such a mess.

Were _____

4 As long as Linda continues to give me a lift to work, I shan't learn to drive.

Were _____

5 Providing his theory isn't disproved, the professor will win the prize.

Were _____

3 Look at this sentence. How is it different to the example sentence in question 1?

Had it rained, the ceremony would have been held indoors.

1 What is the normal sequence of tenses in this type of sentence?

2 What other words can be used to begin this type of sentence?

3 Rewrite the example sentence so that the meaning is the same, but begin with the word *if*.

If _____

4 Finish each of the sentences **1–5** in such a way that it is as similar as possible in meaning to the sentence printed before it.

1 If I'd seen you, I'd have told you about it.

Had _____

2 If the traffic hadn't been so heavy, we'd have arrived in plenty of time.

Had _____

3 Only John's arrival on the scene saved the project from being a complete disaster.

Had _____

4 Were it not to have snowed heavily enough for skiing, a dry ski-run would have been made available.

Had _____

5 As you didn't give notice of your intention to cancel the holiday, the company will not refund your deposit.

Had _____

5 Look at this sentence. How is it different to the previous example sentence?

Should it rain, the ceremony will be held indoors.

1 What is the normal sequence of tenses in this type of sentence?

2 What other words can be used to begin this type of sentence?

3 Rewrite the example sentence so that the meaning is the same, but begin with the word *if*.

If _____

6 Finish each of the sentences **1–5** in such a way that it is as similar as possible in meaning to the sentence printed before it.

1 As long as nobody notices the error, we shall not make an apology.

Should _____

2 If your compact disc proves to be faulty, please return it to the address on the box.

Should _____

3 Were you to lose your ticket, no duplicate would be issued.

Should _____

4 Unless we get held up in the traffic, we'll arrive in time for lunch.

Should _____

5 In the event of a complaint from a customer, the manager must be called directly.

Should _____

LISTENING 2
Sentence completion

1 Discuss these questions with your partner.

At what age do children learn to talk?

What things do they learn first?

How do they learn?

2 You will hear part of an interview with a woman who has written a book on the subject of feral children, children growing up without the company of other human beings. For questions **1–10**, complete the sentences with a word or short phrase.

Many feral children are believed to have been brought up by ⬚ **1** .

Lorna says that she finds many of the stories told about feral children ⬚ **2** .

The sounds made by the wolf girls of Midapur were described as ⬚ **3** .

In eight years one of the girls only managed to learn ⬚ **4** .

Lorna describes the way a baby learns language as a process of ⬚ **5** .

Lorna says it's wrong to liken our language ability to a ⬚ **6** .

Feral children joining human society as teenagers failed to learn ⬚ **7** .

People who learn foreign languages ⬚ **8** are always identifiable as non-native speakers.

Feral children seem to learn vocabulary by means of ⬚ **9** .

Genie failed to learn the language necessary to ⬚ **10** .

3 What does the evidence of feral children tell us about:

- language learning in general?
- learning a foreign language?

PHRASAL VERBS 1

1 Look at these two sentences from the listening text. Underline the phrasal verbs in each one.

We all know people who have taken up foreign languages in adulthood.

It will always be possible to pick up that these are not native speakers.

2 Which of the verbs in the box are closest in meaning to the two phrasal verbs in the example sentences?

started doing   notice   collect   mention   raised   tired   filled

3 Complete each sentence with a suitable verb. Then match the meaning of the phrasal verb you have formed to one of the verbs in the box.

1 I'm _____ up with hearing you complaining, can't you be more positive?

2 Sorry I didn't phone you, but my time has been completely _____ up with a crisis at work.

3 I was _____ up to believe that language learning was about remembering words.

4 Sorry to _____ this up, but didn't you say I might expect a salary rise?

5 I've got to go now because I promised to _____ the children up from school.

WRITING 2
Narratives

1 Think about a day in your childhood when something strange or unusual happened.

1 How much do you remember about each of the following? Make some notes about:
- the weather/time of year
- the place/the event
- the people who were there
- how you felt before anything happened

2 Use your notes to tell your partner about what happened. Ask your partner questions about his/her day.

3 Write a paragraph to introduce the story. This paragraph should describe the background. What will the tense of the main verbs be in this paragraph? What other tenses might you need to use?

2 How much do you remember about the events leading up to this strange or unusual event?

1 How can you make the story more interesting for the reader by building up the scene? Think about:
- what you/others expected to happen that day
- how you were feeling
- the normal things that were happening

2 Write a paragraph that sets the scene for the strange event. What will the main tense of the verbs be in this paragraph? What other tenses might you need to use?

3 How much do you remember about the strange event itself?

1 Do you remember the details that made it strange? Think about:
- how well your readers will understand what happened
- how well they will understand why it was strange
- how well they will understand how you or others felt
- how to tell the story so that the strange thing is surprising

2 Write a paragraph explaining what happened. What will the main tense of the verbs be in this paragraph? What other tenses might you need to use?

3 Think about how you want the story to end. It could be:
- an explanation
- a result
- how you feel now
- what you understand now that you didn't understand then, etc.

4 Write the end of your account.

5 Read through what you have written, checking that the story flows and making any changes you think are necessary.

📖 N.B. The Workbook has further work on narrative tenses.

HELP WITH USE OF ENGLISH: TRANSFORMATIONS 2 ▬▬▬▬

■1 Parts of the Use of English paper asks you to transform sentences from one structure to another. In Paper 3, Question 4 you are given a complete sentence. This is followed by a word in bold.

Example 1:
You should take no notice of your critics.

attention

_____ .

The example needs to be completed like this:

Answer:
You should pay no attention to your critics.

The new sentence must have a similar meaning to the original one, but must use the word in bold in the form it is given; you must not change the word in any way and you must use it in the new sentence.

The new sentence may express the same idea using a different expression, as in example 1, or it may require you to make grammatical changes as in example 2 below. Other changes may also be necessary to complete the new sentence.

Example 2:
Only a small number of people buy the works of this composer.

demand
There is very little demand for the works of this composer.

What has changed? Why?
What has remained the same? Why?
What has been omitted?
What has been added?

Are there any other correct ways to complete the two example transformations?

■2 For each of these transformations, choose the correct answer, **A**, **B** or **C**. Say why the other answers are incorrect.

1 Not everybody likes jazz music.

   taste

   A Jazz music is not to everybody's taste.
   B Not everybody has tasted jazz music.
   C Not everybody has taste in jazz music.

2 Sue is unlikely to get the part in the new film.

   prospect

   A In the new film, Sue has no prospect of getting the part.
   B Sue's prospects of getting a part in the new film are not great.
   C Sue has little prospect of getting the part in the new film.

3 The company has promised to investigate any complaints.

looked

A The company has looked into any complaints.
B The company has promised that any complaints will be looked into.
C The company's promise about complaints was looked into.

4 Duplicate tickets will not be issued for any reason.

account

A On no account will duplicate tickets be issued.
B No account will be taken of duplicate tickets.
C Duplicate tickets will not be issued to any account.

5 The researchers had encountered problems with their camera equipment.

come

A The researchers had come into problems with their camera equipment.
B The researchers' camera equipment had come across problems.
C The researchers had come up against problems with their camera equipment.

▬3 For each of the sentences below, write a new sentence as similar as possible in meaning to the original sentence, but using the word given. This word **must not be altered** in any way.

1 Samantha often talks at length about her own problems.

tendency

_____

2 I don't care what you say, he's got a brilliant analytical mind.

whatever

_____

3 In my opinion, that's not much of a plot for a thriller.

mind

_____

4 The subject matter of that book really makes you think.

provoking

_____

5 This exhibition confirms Lawley's reputation as a great master.

borne

_____

6 I was really surprised to see Sue dressed as Marilyn Monroe at the party.

aback

_____

EXAM PRACTICE 6

◼1 In this section you must choose the word or phrase, **A**, **B**, **C** or **D**, which best completes each sentence.

1 In addition _____ the theories of memory decay, further evidence must be considered.

    A at   **B** to   **C** for   **D** with

2 Any significant mental activity undertaken before or after periods of learning can also account _____ poor retention.

    A at   **B** to   **C** for   **D** with

3 The activities undertaken prior _____ learning may have a detrimental effect on our ability to absorb new input.

    A at   **B** to   **C** for   **D** with

4 Activities undertaken after periods of learning can interfere _____ the effective retention of new input.

    A at   **B** to   **C** for   **D** with

5 This contrasts _____ what is called 'decay' which is more significant in explaining memory failure over a long period of time.

    A at   **B** to   **C** for   **D** with

6 Eighty percent of the information we forget is lost _____ twenty-four hours of our first learning it.

    A within   **B** during   **C** about   **D** away

7 This may help to explain why testing activities carried _____ the day after the lesson may yield rather distressing results.

    A away   **B** out   **C** forward   **D** off

8 The rate at which we forget clearly has implications _____ revision and recycling of the information we have to learn.

    A for   **B** from   **C** to   **D** towards

9 Most of you will be familiar _____ the experience of forgetting a friend's telephone number.

    A to   **B** for   **C** with   **D** at

10 An interesting case of a feral child has recently _____ to light.

    A got   **B** began   **C** taken   **D** come

2 Fill each of the numbered blanks in the passage with **one** suitable word.

Why do we forget?

In spite of the remarkable efficiency of the human brain, we still suffer (**1**) _____ lapses of memory when we are (**2**) _____ to remember something that we thought was well established in our mind. Why does this happen?

One theory of forgetting suggests that information stored in the memory falls (**3**) _____ disuse unless it (**4**) _____ activated fairly regularly. In other words, we need to practise and revise (**5**) _____ we have learnt, otherwise the new input (**6**) _____ gradually fade in the memory and ultimately disappear. (**7**) _____ is called 'decay theory'.

(**8**) _____ opposition to this theory is the idea (**9**) _____ 'cue-dependent forgetting', which asserts that information does in (**10**) _____ persist in the memory but we may be unable to recall it. In other words, the failure is (**11**) _____ of retrieval rather than storage. Evidence for this theory derives (**12**) _____ a number of experiments.

In one (**13**) _____, subjects were given lists of words to learn and then tested (**14**) _____ their powers of recall. (**15**) _____ they were tested again, only this (**16**) _____ they were given relevant information to facilitate recall. For example, (**17**) _____ a list contained the words 'sofa', 'armchair' and 'wardrobe', the subjects would be given the superordinate 'furniture' (**18**) _____ a cue to help them. These experiments showed that recall was considerably strengthened (**19**) _____ appropriate retrieval cues, (**20**) _____ suggesting that the information was not permanently lost but only mislaid.

3 Fill each of the blanks with a suitable word or phrase.

1 As luck _____, the phone rang just as I had got into the bath.

2 Whatever is that man's name? Oh dear, it's on the _____, but I can't remember it.

3 The experience of feeling you're being watched is by _____ an uncommon one; in fact it happens a lot.

4 It is hoped that Mr Sheldrake's forthcoming experiment will throw further _____ the question.

5 You need to know the first letter of the word, because they are listed _____ order.

4   Finish each of the following sentences in such a way that it is as similar as possible in meaning to the sentence printed before it.

Example: Immediately after his departure, things improved.

Answer: No sooner *had he departed than things improved.*

1   Unless you remember to take your invitation, the doorman will not let you in.
Were _____

2   As you did not pay the bill on time, you are not entitled to a discount.
Were _____

3   As you didn't give me your address, I was unable to write to you.
Had _____

4   The more complex the problem is, the harder your brain works.
If _____

5   After reading each sentence, they were asked a question about it.
Once _____

6   The brain achieves more if it works harder.
The harder _____

7   Let me know if you are in need of any help.
Should _____

8   If you practise your driving more often, you will be more likely to pass the test.
The more _____

9   The only way to stop global warming is by concerted international action
Only through _____

10 Only a large government grant allowed the school to buy a multi-media centre.
Had it _____

A Matter of Taste

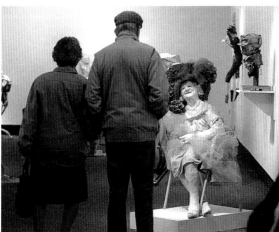

SPEAKING 1
Expressing opinions

1 Discuss these questions with your partner.

What is good taste?
- how can you tell?
- who decides what is good taste?
- is good taste important?

2 Read the words in the box. Discuss how they relate to ideas of good taste. Then look at the four photographs. Compare and contrast them using as many ideas from the box as you can.

art	culture
design	elegance
fashion	individuality
originality	style

☐ LISTENING 1

Matching

▥ 1 Before you listen answer these questions.

1 How important do you think each of the following factors is in determining our taste in things?

age	class	education	gender	experience
aspirations	occupation	race	nationality	wealth

2 Look at the pictures. Which objects appear feminine to you, which masculine and which seem to have no particular gender?

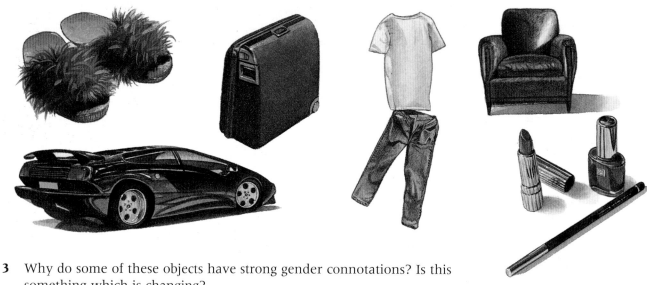

3 Why do some of these objects have strong gender connotations? Is this something which is changing?

▥ 2 You will hear part of a radio programme in which two designers are asked their views on the subject of gender and taste. For questions **1–8**, decide which of the speakers expresses this view. Write **V** for Vivian, **D** for Darren or **B** for both of them.

1 Gender is probably the most important factor influencing a person's taste.   **1** ☐

2 We immediately recognize objects as either masculine or feminine.   **2** ☐

3 Many of our ideas about the gender of objects have their roots in the very distant past.   **3** ☐

4 These days our stereotyped ideas are changing fast.   **4** ☐

5 In the past, feminine taste was held in high esteem.   **5** ☐

6 Ideas of 'design' rather than 'taste' have challenged women's traditional roles.   **6** ☐

7 People are now more likely to make personal choices rather than follow stereotypes.   **7** ☐

8 We cannot say whether the relationship between gender and taste will change in the future.   **8** ☐

3 How did the speakers express agreement and disagreement? Listen again to these phrases from the listening. In each case, is the speaker agreeing or disagreeing? The first one is an example.

1	*agree*	5	_____	9	_____
2	_____	6	_____	10	_____
3	_____	7	_____		
4	_____	8	_____		

Do you think goods will continue to have gender connotations? Use some of the words and expressions from the listening in your discussion. Agree and disagree with your partner as appropriate.

VOCABULARY 1
Part One
Adjectives

Look at these words from the listening. Which would you use to talk about:

- men
- women
- places
- objects
- language

cluttered	cosy	flowery	efficient	eclectic	imaginative
rational	pretentious	original	superficial	fluffy	

Part Two
Synonyms

1 Darren believes the issue of gender is 'central to' ideas of taste. What would be a good synonym for 'central to' in this context?

2 For questions **1–6** find a suitable synonym for each of the highlighted parts of these words or phrases.

1 gender is **ingrained in our consciousness**
2 gender differences have become **blurred**
3 everything's **up for grabs** these days
4 fixed **stereotypes** remain actually
5 you can no longer **generalize** like that
6 people don't feel so **hidebound** by these images any longer

Comprehension

1

1 What type of person do you imagine owning works of art?

2 Do you think works of art are worth the money that people pay for them?

3 Why do people buy works of art?

2 Read the article about the owner of the picture by the late 19th century French painter, Cezanne, and answer the questions which follow it.

HOW TO LIVE WITH YOUR OWN CEZANNE

*Walking around the Cezanne exhibition in London, one starts to wonder, after the eighth room of masterpieces, where all these pictures come from. One knows **Les Grandes Baigneuses** from the National Gallery, but some of the paintings are complete strangers, flown in from São Paolo, St Petersburg, Ohio, Canberra and Cardiff. And then there is a smattering of works marked 'private collection'. Despite their being 226 works in the show, there is only one belonging to a private owner that actually reveals the name on the label. This is Le Bassin du Jas de Bouffan in gallery 4. It is a small to medium-sized work, painted between 1878 and 1880, and it is owned by Madame Corinne Cuellar.*

It is not a particularly crowd-pleasing work, as many of Cezanne's landscapes are. Painted in winter at his father's grand but neglected weekend retreat, it has a stark, geometric quality that could be overshadowed by the more brightly appealing views of *L'Estaque* hanging on either side. But *Le Monde* has run a half-page appreciation of this Cezanne and the exhibition picks it out as pivotal in the artist's 'constructive' phase. Yet, it usually hangs in a small dining-room.

Madame Cuellar has never given an interview about her Cezanne before. In an age when art thieves treat security systems with contempt, you can't blame her. But after the intervention of a chain of five people, she and her husband agree to meet me in a hotel.

People who own big pictures tend to have big hair, big coats and shoes that aren't made for walking, but for separating their feet from the limousine carpet. By contrast, Madame Cuellar, a medium-sized woman in her late thirties, has mousey hair and is wearing a well-cut, but hardly arresting black jacket. Her husband, Arturo, looks equally low-profile in a green coat, although he is wearing a bow-tie for identification purposes, which is lucky. Otherwise we'd still be circling the hotel lobby.

The first thing to be negotiated was what I could say and what I couldn't say 'for security reasons'. In interviews one usually refrains from mentioning the street in which someone lives. Just occasionally, one fudges which village. But the Cuellars would rather I brushed over which continent they come from. All they will say is that they live in one of four flats in a converted house. 'We don't have sleepless nights about security... really we don't, otherwise there would be no pleasure in owning it.'

They have only owned the picture since 1992 when Madame Cuellar bought it at an auction in London, after seeing it in Paris when it was on a whistle-stop tour to drum up buyers.

For Madame Cuellar, the effect was instant. 'I had seen it in reproduction, but when I saw it close up, I thought, "I love this painting." It was not just because it was by Cezanne. For me it is a key work, which makes the bridge between the 19th and 20th centuries, but it was the atmosphere in the work that is so amazing, you can really feel the air and the lightness. There have been few things that have touched me in that way... not for years and years.'

The work had been in the collection of the Pellerin family who bought it in 1909, and it had hung in their mansion in Neuilly for nearly 80 years. Madame Cuellar bid for it herself, and the hammer went down at £1.4 million, which she clearly thinks is quite cheap for a Cezanne. And, as art dealers remember only too well, 1992 was a year when prices went into free-fall. Still, the *International Herald Tribune* described it as the best buy of the year. The Cuellars think, in a typically understated way: 'We were quite lucky. With auctions one never knows.'

Needless to say, you need more than cash to buy a Cezanne. One also needs considerable courage to lay out a vast sum for what Madame Cuellar calls 'just paint on a bit of canvas'. Almost inevitably, she comes from a dynasty of art dealers while she herself is a paper restorer. Arturo, whom she met in London while they were both studying there, is a dealer in Old Master drawings. One gets a clear sense that they buy works for their eclectic-sounding collection together.

The refreshing feature of the Cuellars is that they seem to have bought their Cezanne because they genuinely loved it. This is rarer than one might think. When I ask them if they take people around their flat like sightseers, Mme Cuellar gives a blank uncomprehending frown. 'We don't have the painting for a social reason, it's so that we can build up a personal relationship with it.' They don't hold cocktail parties in front of it then? 'Oh no, many of our friends don't even realize it's there.'

The Cuellars don't have a car, a big villa or a swimming pool, and their two sons go to the local state school. When I see them later at the exhibition, they were looking at their painting. Neither of them can wait to get it back. As Mme Cuellar says: 'It's good that lots of people can see it, but without it our house has a different atmosphere. It's like being without a good friend.'

1 Why was the writer first attracted to this particular painting in the exhibition?

2 Which word in paragraph one gives the idea of a small number, evenly distributed?

3 In your own words, explain why the painting is less 'crowd-pleasing' than other pictures by Cezanne.

4 Which word in paragraph two tells us how important this example of Cezannne's work is.

5 How are the Cuellars different from most owners of valuable works of art?

6 In your own words, explain why it was fortunate that Mr Cuellar was wearing a bow-tie?

7 Which words in paragraph five describe how the writer usually tries to protect the people he interviews?

8 In your own words, explain when and why the picture was taken to Paris.

9 What does Madame Cuellar mean when she describes the painting as 'a bridge'?

10 Why was 1992 a good year to buy a painting?

11 Which words in paragraph eight describe things that happen at an auction?

12 What two things do you need in order to buy a Cezanne?

13 Why does the writer begin the section about Madme Cuellar's family with the words 'almost inevitably'?

14 What is Madame Cuellar keen to deny in the final two paragraphs?

HELP WITH SUMMARY WRITING

In Section B of the Use of English paper you are asked to write a summary of one aspect of the reading passage you have read. The following section will help you to develop the skills of summarizing the main points.

1 Look back through the article and mark all the sections which tell us about why Madame Cuellar chose this painting for her dining-room.

2 Compare your notes with another student; did you find the same points?

3 Make a list of the points in your own words.

4 Decide which points are the most important and put them into the most logical order.

5 How can the points be linked together e.g. firstly, secondly etc.?

6 In a paragraph of around 80–100 words, summarize the reasons why Madame Cuellar chose this painting to buy for her dining-room.

7 Look at this summary which a student wrote in answer to the question above.

- Does it include the same points that you made?
- Are the points in the same order?
- How have the points been linked together?
- How has the student avoided repeating words and phrases?
- What type of words/structures has the student used to keep the points concise?

> *Mme Cuellar first saw the painting in Paris and fell in love with it. She didn't buy it just because it was a Cezanne, though she acknowledges its importance as a central work which bridges the nineteenth and twentieth centuries. She bought it because she loved the atmosphere of the painting and because it moved her. She denies that she bought it to show off to her friends, saying instead that she wanted to build a personal relationship with it. It seems that the writer of the article is convinced that her claim is genuine.*

REMEMBER

1 When writing a summary,

- collect points from different parts of the passage
- only use information from the passage, not your own ideas
- check the rubric to make sure that all the points you include are relevant
- make sure you have included all the relevant points
- don't copy sentences from the passage, but rewrite the points in your own words
- make sure that the points you make are linked together in a logical way
- remember that marks are awarded for:

a selecting the relevant points, and
b the language you use to write the summary

2 Further practice. Look back at the article and plan another summary with a different focus. Some of the points may be the same as those you used before, whilst others will be different. Look at the rubric carefully. How is the focus different?

In a paragraph of 60–80 words, summarize the reasons why, in the writer's view, Madame Cuellar is unlike many other owners of works of art.

SPEAKING 2
Developing a topic

1 Look at these pictures. Talk to your partner about why you like or dislike each one.

Think about:

subject matter	images portrayed	use of colour
skill of the artist	what it makes you think of	
how it makes you feel	who it might appeal to	

2 Look at these two passages. Read them both and then compare and contrast them, saying:

- where you think each of them comes from
- the style in which they are written
- the ideas they put forward

Passage 1

At the end of February, the gallery unveils one of the most lavish gifts in its history – Janet Walton's collection of 56 works of contemporary art, worth an estimated $23 million. It is a donation that will greatly expand the scope of the gallery's 20th century collection. The gift may be unusual in scale, but not unusual in its effect. Although in many countries we tend to think of art as being publicly funded, it is the private collector who has formed its base, corrected its weaknesses and directed its taste.

Passage 2

IF YOU THOUGHT you could never afford to buy contemporary art, think again. 'Over the next three years, the art market will change beyond all recognition,' says Deborah Petley of the Art Supermarket, which is in the vanguard of the new movement in art retailing. The Art supermarket, on the fifth floor of a fashionable New York store, next to the restaurant, has sold over 3000 paintings in the space of 14 months. A high turnover and low overheads means that prices can be half those of conventional art dealers, who, in turn, are now slashing their prices by coming out of their galleries and into a store near you.

3 Imagine that you have to choose a picture or poster for either your wall at home, your classroom or the place where you work. Talk about how important some of the following points would be when choosing a picture. Which points would be more important in the different situations?

- size
- colour
- subject matter
- style of drawing/painting/graphics
- reputation of the artist
- how fashionable it is
- what your family/friends think of it
- how much you like it
- the message/idea it communicates
- how much it costs

USE OF ENGLISH 1
Cloze passage

1 Before you complete the cloze passage discuss these questions with your partner.

1 What do you know about the artist John Constable?

2 Do you like his work?

3 Why do you think his work is popular?

4 What do you think about famous artists' work being used on souvenirs or for advertising?

2 Fill each of the numbered blanks in the pasage with **one** suitable word. The first one has been done for you as an example.

The Naffing of Constable

'At home with Constable's Cornfield' at the National Gallery is (**0**) __*the*__ worst exhibition to be put (**1**) _____ there for a very long time. It would be an eyesore anywhere; in the (**2**) _____ of Britain's finest picture collection (**3**) _____ is a scandal. Constable's popular painting is surrounded (**4**) _____ reproductions of it on china, tea-trays, wallpapers, biscuit tins, etc., as (**5**) _____ as the copied daubs of Sunday painters.

Some people may (**6**) _____ of the idea, saying 'Why not show the love ordinary people have (**7**) _____ this picture?' or 'It brings in the sort of people who (**8**) _____ otherwise not come.'

But (**9**) _____ is not the purpose of the National Gallery. Its function is to banish sentimental thinking and maintain the highest standards. (**10**) _____ is such elitism shunned in polite artistic society (**11**) _____ in sport, for example, nothing else matters? To exhibit tea-trays at the National Gallery is like (**12**) _____ the canteen staff represent Manchester United in the Cup – no football fan (**13**) _____ tolerate such a sacrilege (**14**) _____ in his worst nightmare.

Yet for admirers of Constable the nightmare (**15**) _____ arrived. One of the worst consequences (**16**) _____ showing the picture in this way is that it drags it (**17**) _____ . Engulfed by trash, *The Cornfield* does not look so good.

Educational the exhibition is not. All it (**18**) _____ is that most people have appalling taste. By including photographs of owners and objects in (**19**) _____ homes, insult is (**20**) _____ to injury. The very people the exhibition intends to please are made to look silly.

3 Which of the following words do you think best describes the writer's attitude?

arrogant   indignant   patronizing   scornful
condescending   exasperated   disappointed   measured

4 What do you think the role of art galleries should be?

READING 2 ▊▊▊▊▊▊▊▊▊▊▊▊▊▊▊▊▊▊▊▊▊▊▊▊▊▊▊▊▊▊▊▊▊▊▊▊▊
Part One
Multiple choice

▬ 1   You are going to read part of a novel about a large house in the country
where a group of artists live. People interested in learning artistic skills come
for short residential courses at the house. The novel is set in the 1970s.

1   What styles do you associate with the 1970s? Think about: music, art,
fashion, design, etc.

2   What type of people do you think the artists are?

▬ 2   Read this extract from the novel.

FRAMLEIGH HOUSE

Two hours later, the visitors have been allocated their rooms, have unpacked their bags and learned their way about the place. They have met Toby, the owner, Paula and other members of the Framleigh Artistic Community; they have discovered the studios and the Common Room and the refectory, wandered out onto the terrace and along the prospect
10 and back along the overgrown paths of the old kitchen garden. They have been impressed, bemused or affronted by the place according to age, inclination and experience. None of them remains unmoved, since Framleigh is, in its way, unique.

Designed by William Kent, the house itself is perhaps not outstanding. There are other eighteenth century country
20 houses of equal or greater grace and elegance. But the park has always been considered a masterpiece, transcended only by Rousham and Stowe, the perfect manifestation of the picturesque: Hogarthian lines of beauty, sham ruins, cascades, grotto, the lot. Twenty-five acres in which the disordered was cunningly turned into a contrivance, in which the physical world was made an
30 artistic product, in which nature became art.

All that, though, was a long time ago, and since then much has happened including the misfortune of several generations of Standishes. Toby's father

failed to take advantage of the opportunities offered by mass tourism and Framleigh has gone to seed. What the course members see, as they wander
40 about the place, is a lamentable ruin of what was, overlaid by the tastes of subsequent generations: by Victorian brick, by Edwardian insensitivity, and above all by weeds.

Elegance is now at so many removes as to seem not so much irretrievable as barely to be imagined. In the Common Room – once the drawing room – hangs an oil painting of the house in its hey-day, spruce
50 and sparkling in a landscape clean as a whistle, the trees and grass manicured, the parterre precise as an architectural diagram. Indeed, there is something diagrammatic about the whole painting, not least the bewigged and beribboned figures parading in the foreground, doll-like men and women, impossible to think of as flesh and blood. Thus, too, the house's own previous persona seems fictional, a
60 mythical thing from the pages of a book, its present blurred and muted state far more real and apposite.

In the painting, the houses and park appear as a contrived and ordered island amid the green ocean of the countryside. In contrast, today, the shaggy woodland of Kent's landscaped grounds is an unexpected tumult amongst the disciplined squares and oblongs of
70 agricultural Warwickshire. Many of the trees, of course, have far outgrown the intended scale; elsewhere undergrowth

PENELOPE LIVELY

NEXT TO NATURE, ART

'An abundance of fun'
– Sunday Telegraph

and copses have blunted the original layout; the serpentine lake has all but vanished in thickets of unquenchable rhododendron. The whole place appears to be held in check only by the estate wall: a disorderly raffish presence alongside the innocent council houses and bungalows
80 displaying their washing, greenhouses and prams where village and the entrance to Framleigh Park meet at the road.

In the same way, the inside of the house has an atmosphere not so much of graceful decay as an insensitivity to change, a kind of deafness and blindness to the world that saddles it now with peeling wallpapers, old flooring shivered into a spider's web of cracks, wheezing
90 pipes, clanking sanitation and a pervasive smell of damp. Since Toby, when up against it, has sold off most of the remaining paintings and the better pieces of furniture, the rooms are furnished with thirties stuff giving way to modern in the 'visitors' bedrooms and an element of ethnic cushions, rugs and covers introduced lately by Paula.

From Next to Nature, Art

3 Now answer the questions **1-6**. Choose the answer **A**, **B**, **C** or **D** which you think fits best.

1 What is the visitor's first reaction to Framleigh House?

   A They are all equally impressed by it.
   B They have each felt a strong reaction to it.
   C They have all found it difficult to appreciate.
   D They have each found different things to admire.

2 Why is the writer so impressed by the park?

   A It is better than any other.
   B It is in perfect harmony with the house.
   C It shows the beauty of natural things.
   D It was designed as a work of art.

3 What has caused Framleigh to lose its original elegance?

   A changes of ownership
   B tasteless alterations
   C poor maintenance
   D the effects of tourism

4 How does the writer feel about the painting in the Common Room?

   A It is not well painted.
   B It doesn't seem realistic.
   C It seems out of place there.
   D It may be genuine.

5 How does Framleigh Park now look different from the painting of it in the Common Room?

   A It no longer looks so well proportioned.
   B It no longer contrasts with the surrounding countryside.
   C It is no longer isolated from the village.
   D It no longer has a clearly defined boundary.

6 Why has Toby changed some of the furnishings at Framleigh House?

   A to reflect its new use
   B to bring it up to date
   C for aesthetic reasons
   D for financial reasons

Part Two
Comprehension

■ 1 Now read the extract again and answer these questions.

1 Which three words in paragraph one indicate ways in which the visitors are different to one another?

2 Which two nouns in paragraph two describe the house?

3 Why are 'Rousham' and Stowe' mentioned in paragraph two?

4 What is 'All that' referred to in line 32?

5 What word in paragraph three tells us most about the history of the Standish family?

6 Which idiomatic phrase in paragraph three describes what has happened to Framleigh in recent years?

7 Which word in paragraph three gives us a sad impression of Framleigh?

8 What do you think is meant by Framleigh's 'hey-day'? (line 49)

9 Which idiomatic phrase in paragraph four is also a simile?

10 What does the writer mean by 'flesh and blood'? (line 58)

11 Which word in paragraph four means 'in the right place'?

12 What metaphor is used for Framleigh and the surrounding countryside in paragraph five?

13 In what sense do you think the rhododendrons are 'unquenchable'? (line 75)

14 Which phrase in paragraph five means 'kept under control'?

15 The estate wall is described as ' disorderly' and 'raffish' in line 78. What do you think it looks like?

16 Which two adjectives in paragraph six describe noises?

17 In what sense do you think the cushions, rugs and covers are 'ethnic'? (line 97)

VOCABULARY 2 ▮▮▮▮▮▮▮▮▮▮▮▮▮▮▮▮▮▮▮▮▮▮▮▮▮
Prefixes

Look at these three words from the extract. What do they have in common?

a overgrown (line 10)
b outgrown (line 71)
c undergrowth (line 72)

Which is a noun
          an adjective
          a verb?

Can you find any other examples of words formed in this way in the text?

Complete each sentence with a word formed with *out*, *over* or *under*.

1 There has been an _____ of food poisoning amongst the hotel's guests.

2 She always says what she thinks, she's very _____ .

3 The accident happened when the car was trying to _____ a lorry.

4 The factory's _____ has more than doubled in the past eighteen months.

5 Your landlady will wash small items like _____ , larger things must go to the laundry.

📖 N.B. The Workbook has further work on prefixes.

GRAMMAR 1
Inversions

1 Look at this sentence from the passage.

Designed by William Kent, the house itself is not outstanding.

1 What is the subject of the sentence?
2 Why did the writer decide to begin the sentence in this way?
3 Rewrite the sentence so that it begins with the subject.
4 How many ways are there of writing the sentence so that the subject comes first?

2 Rewrite the following sentences so that they do not begin with the subject.

1 Bob, who is a competent potter, would be equally good at making chairs or clocks.

_____

2 The pottery group, which is by far the most popular, meets on Mondays.

_____

3 Paula, who feels at ease with all kinds of people, is a mixture of successful businesswoman and artist.

_____

3 Now, look at these sentences.

'So happy was Toby feeling that he forgot about his troubles.'

'Beautiful as the garden may be, it doesn't compare with Rousham.'

1 What is the subject in each of these sentences?
2 Rewrite them so that they begin with the subject.

_____

_____

3 How are they different from each other?

4 Rewrite each of the following sentences so that they do not begin with the subject.

1 Nick was so interested by the course, he decided to change his career.

_____

2 Valerie's work was so good that she was offered a pay rise.

_____

3 John's painting is impressive, but it's not in the same class as Paula's.

_____

4 The course may have been enjoyable, but I'm afraid it wasn't worth the money.

_____

📖 N.B. The Workbook has further work on inversions.

🎧 LISTENING 2
Note completion

1 Before you listen discuss these questions with your partner.

1 What type of work do graphic designers do?

2 How is the work of a graphic designer different to that of a portrait or landscape painter?

3 How much are you influenced by the design of products and packaging when you buy things?

2

Part One

You will hear part of a radio programme about the designs which appear on disposable kitchen towels. For questions **1–7**, complete the notes with a word or short phrase.

A few words on kitchen towels

Kitchen towel attributes:

- design

- colour

- [_____ 1]

- absorbency

- environmentally friendly

[_____ 2] of purchasing decisions linked to design.

Tests show that housewives often like [_____ 3] .

Client gives designer idea of required design, e.g. floral, [_____ 4] or pictorial.

Recent years: [_____ 5] more important in kitchen design.

Increased use of colour demanded by [_____ 6] .

Designers themselves tend to prefer [_____ 7] .

Part Two

Each of the designers goes on to talk about one design found on paper towels. As you listen, look at the five designs below and write the speaker's name under the picture each is referring to.

1

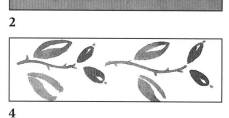

2

4

3

5

SPEAKING 3
Comparing and contrasting

1 Look at these pictures of rooms.

A

2 Describe the rooms labelled **A** and **B** by saying what is similar and what is different about them. Talk about:

- choice of furniture/fabrics/ornaments/decorations, etc.

- arrangement of furniture, etc.

- choice of colours, textures, etc.

- lighting

Who do you think lives in such a room?

Would you like to live there?

What are the advantages/disadvantages of the room?

What changes would you make to the room?

B

WRITING 1
Giving opinions

The composition paper sometimes includes a question which asks you to take two ideas and relate them to each other as you write. This type of composition needs careful planning. The following exercises are designed to help you.

1 Think of someone you know very well, for example your best friend, a family member, your partner, even yourself.

1 Make a list of words to describe this person under these headings.

Physical appearance   Character   Lifestyle

2 Now think of something which reflects that person's taste, for example:
- their taste in clothes
- their room, flat or house
- their car or other prized possession
- a picture or other artistic object

Make a list of words and phrases to describe the thing(s) you have chosen.

3 Look for connections between the two lists. In particular things which may be surprising, unexpected or interesting.

2 Read this composition title.

To what extent does the choice of the material things we surround ourselves with reflect our personality and attitude to life?

This type of composition is asking for your opinion and needs to include examples to support the points you make.

1 First think about the basic idea presented in the question and decide whether you wish to:
- agree with it;
- disagree with it;
- discuss it without coming to a conclusion.

2 Now think about how to use your examples which should be taken from your lists above. You could, for instance:
- compare yourself with another person/ other people
- give real-life examples of someone/people you know
- use your ideas to talk about people in general/types of people

3 Now think about the structure of your composition. It will need an introduction, three to four paragraphs and a conclusion.

What will you include in your introduction?
What main point will you have in each paragraph?
What examples will you include to support this point?

Remember your paragraphs should be leading to your conclusion.

- What will you include in your conclusion?

4 Think about the language that you will use in the composition. For example:

Exemplification
My brother is a good example of this. He …
Consider the example of my cousin, Louisa. She …
You only have to look at the average teenager to see …

Concession
Although we tend to think that …
Despite the fact that …

Surprising/Unsurprising information
Far from being conservative in his choice of music, X is rather adventurous.
As I had expected, she chose the …
Strange as it may seem, his room is actually quite …
Her choice of X was exactly what I would have expected/predicted
Contrary to my expectations, Jill chose …

Useful words and expressions
It's the exception which proves the rule
stereotypes
generalize
keen on
fond of
a (great) fan of
to do what is expected
to follow fashion

---

5 Now write your composition. Use the words and expressions in the boxes to help you. Write no more than 350 words.

EXAM PRACTICE 7

1 In this section, you must choose the word or phrase **A**, **B**, **C**, or **D** which best completes each sentence.

1 Two hours later, the visitors had been _____ their rooms.

    A allocated   **B** apportioned   **C** designated   **D** delegated

2 Toby's father failed to _____ advantage of the possibilities of mass tourism.

    A make   **B** take   **C** get   **D** catch

3 A feminine environment is typically pictured as cosy and _____ .

    A smattered   **B** spattered   **C** littered   **D** cluttered

4 In recent years, distinctions between male and female clothes have become _____ .

    A fudged   **B** smeared   **C** blurred   **D** smudged

5 The painting usually _____ in Madame Cuellar's dining-room.

    A hangs   **B** rests   **C** exhibits   **D** shows

6 In articles, I usually _____ from mentioning where interviewees live.

    A refuse   **B** avoid   **C** renounce   **D** refrain

7 These days, art thieves _____ security systems with contempt.

    A consider   **B** deem   **C** behold   **D** treat

8 The house is very old and there is a _____ smell of damp.

    A common   **B** rife   **C** pervasive   **D** diffuse

9 Arturo was wearing a bow-tie for the _____ of identification.

    A functions   **B** purposes   **C** motives   **D** reasons

10 I can't _____ patterns on paper towels, they're awful.

    A affirm   **B** assent   **C** abide   **D** accord

2 Fill each of the numbered spaces in the passage with **one** suitable word.

Daughter of the iron house

Today Pat Smith is returning to the house where she was born, slightly surprised to discover it has become a museum piece. When she was born in 1927, the house in Dudley looked like (**1**) _____ other semi-detached house in England, (**2**) _____ there were two clues to how it was different; its name, *The Iron House*, and the consequences when a child couldn't (**3**) _____ the temptation and hurled a stone, it clanged (**4**) _____ a gong when struck.

In fact, three pairs of cast-iron semis were built in Dudley. It (**5**) _____ thought they would be cheap and easy to build and they were indeed quick to assemble – records (**6**) _____ that the 600 cast-iron panels for these houses were bolted (**7**) _____ in eight days. But in the (**8**) _____ they cost nearly twice as much as brick, and (**9**) _____ the experiment ended.

Now there is only one pair (**10**) _____ , jigsawed together at the Black Country Museum, Dudley, (**11**) _____ of the best bits of the six houses. One of the houses is (**12**) _____ le with stripped interior walls to reveal the construction, and the (**13**) _____ fitted out (**14**) _____ original furniture, painstakingly refurbished to look brand new.

The museum has found the original plans and contracts and discovered a (**15**) _____ of social engineering built (**16**) _____ the design. The houses had big front rooms and deliberately small kitchens, in the hope that people (**17**) _____ sit in the front rooms (**18**) _____ than the kitchen, and occupy (**19**) _____ with improving hobbies.

Mrs Smith remembers the house with great affection. 'It was a lovely house', she says, 'people say they were cold in the winter and like an oven in the summer, but I don't remember (**20**) _____ .I'm delighted it's in the museum – I shall take my grandchildren to see it'.

3 Fill each of the blanks with a suitable word or phrase.
1 I have no idea who will win the prize; everything _____ grabs.
2 The old house is a ruin, it's really _____ seed in recent years.
3 The origins of the ancient ceremony are lost in _____ of time.
4 The garden has gone wild, only the old wall _____ check.
5 His attempts to apologize were so inept they added _____ injury.

4 For each of the sentences below, write a new sentence as similar as possible in meaning to the original sentence, but using the word given. This word **must not be altered** in any way.

Example: A lot of people attended the meeting.

        turnout

Answer: *There was a very poor turnout for the meeting.*

1 Seeing that picture reminded me of holidays in Cornwall.
brought

2 It takes great courage to invest a vast sum in a picture.
lay

3 John went to Paris to get people interested in the scheme.
drum

4 I have visited other old houses with greater grace and elegance.
most

5 His requests to have the flooring renewed were not listened to.
deaf

6 I don't think we should seek to excuse Paula's rude behaviour.
allowances

7 I must say that the idea of visiting an artistic community has never appealed to me.
fancied

8 It was assumed that Roy would live in the house he inherited from his father.
granted

9 The lecture failed to live up to Deirdre's expectations.
fell

10 The hotel makes every effort to ensure the safety and comfort of guests.
lengths

5 Finish each of the following sentences in such a way that it is as similar as possible in meaning to the sentence printed before it.

Example: Immediately after his departure, things improved.

Answer: No sooner *had he departed than things improved.*

1 Danny's fed up with the fact that Susan always plays such loud music.
Danny wishes _____

2 It is believed that the stolen paintings are hidden in a mountain cave.
The stolen _____

3 I'd have preferred learning carpentry at school instead of history of art.
I'd rather _____

4 The garden gave the appearance of having been untended for years.
The garden looked _____

5 The gallery can only deal with a limited number of visitors at any one time.
There is a _____

6 I had no idea that Ruby's portrait was on display in that exhibition.
It came as _____

7 'I'm sorry, I know nothing about architecture' said Polly.
Polly admitted to _____

8 Graphic design and fine art require an equal amount of skill.
Just as much _____

9 Graham's expert advice was the thing which helped me to realize my potential as an artist.
If it _____

10 The potters finally managed to buy their own studio only after years of saving.
Only _____

Go your own Way

VOCABULARY 1
Advertising

1 Talk to your partner about advertising. Think about:

- different types of advertising
- the best way/place to advertise these products and services

food	banking services	detergents
clothes	children's toys	cosmetics
local events	music concerts	insurance

- an advertisement you think is effective – say why
- an advertisement you especially like or dislike – say why

2 Fill each of the numbered blanks in the passage with **one** suitable word from the box. The first one has been done for you as an example.

artwork	audience	brands	campaigns	catalogue
circulation	consumers	leaflets	mailing	media
medium	multinational	~~place~~	production	rates
research	revolution	samples	space	traders
up-market				

Advertising

The modern market (**0**) __*place*__ contains a bewildering choice of goods, all competing for our attention. Manufacturers are advertising to inform us about their products and persuade us to buy them. Throughout history, each new development in communications has led to a new type of advertising. Street (**1**) _____ have always had special cries to alert people to their presence, and the development of printing made newspaper advertisements possible. The industrial (**2**) _____ of the 19th century led to mass (**3**) _____ of goods, and the 20th century provided the mass communication of radio and television to sell them.

Now that (**4**) _____ companies do business across the globe, their products are referred to as world (**5**) _____ . Advertising them is a costly affair and has effects on the lives of people in many countries.

Each different means of advertising is called a (**6**) _____ – a way of getting information across. By choosing the right ones, a business can reach the (**7**) _____ most likely to want or be able to afford its product. Market (**8**) _____ companies help a business to decide if these people read a publication or watch a television programme which might carry its advertisements.

A small business might wish to send (**9**) _____ to people in their homes, letting locals know where to find it. Those dealing with expensive (**10**) _____ items can buy a (**11**) _____ list of prosperous homes from a list broker and post direct mail material to particular addresses. Some companies advertise their goods in a mail order (**12**) _____ , a booklet showing products available by post. Advertising (**13**) _____ can be bought in local newspapers and radio channels.

Larger organizations opt for national or international advertising. National newspapers have a very wide (**14**) _____ and charge high (**15**) _____ for advertising. Glossy magazines print elegant colour (**16**) _____ to show off goods and sometimes give away small packets of products as (**17**) _____ .

The most widely recognized advertisements appear on television. They reach a large (**18**) _____ in a very receptive situation. Big manufacturers use various (**19**) _____ in an organized series of advertisements called (**20**) _____ which are worked out by advertising agencies.

SPEAKING 1
Discussing values

1 What are the responsibilities of advertisers? Talk about:

- honesty/good taste/accuracy
- effects on people's lifestyles
- effects on people's expectations
- effects on people's expenditure
- effects on children

2 What do you understand by these terms?

merchandising   marketing   brand loyalty   trade marks   spin-offs

3 Look at these advertisements.

How effective do you think each one is?
How does it achieve its effect?

LISTENING 1
Part One
Matching

1 Before you listen, discuss these questions with your partner.

1 Have you ever played computer games? Talk to your partner about:

- What games you like/don't like

- What images/stereotypes do you think are portrayed in games? For example:
good/bad
male/female
winning/losing
competition/collaboration

- Who you think designs the games?

- What type of people the games are designed for?

- What, if any, is the educational value of games?

2 You will hear three young people talking about computer games. Which of the statements **A–F** best summarizes the main point each person is making?

A the games are too violent

B the games are improving

C the games are very predictable

D the games allow no choice of hero

E the games reflect real life

F the games use unfair stereotypes

Person 1 _____

Person 2 _____

Person 3 _____

Part Two

1 You will now hear two people being interviewed: Claire, a mathematics professor, and Nick, a computer game designer. They will be talking about computer games. For questions **1–9**, decide which of the two speakers expresses each point of view. Write **C** for Claire, **N** for Nick or **B** for both of them.

1 The students' attitudes matched my predictions. 1 ☐

2 Some attempts have been made to make games more attractive to girls. 2 ☐

3 Some people doubt the value of the games in any case. 3 ☐

4 The nature of the games may be a factor affecting people's career choices. 4 ☐

5 The makers of the games have found a very lucrative market. 5 ☐

6 Attempts to make a special game for girls seem appropriate. 6 ☐

7 Women fighters in games are a welcome development. 7 ☐

8 Computer games should have an educational purpose. 8 ☐

9 The best games are those which everyone can play equally. 9 ☐

VOCABULARY 2
Writing definitions

1 Look at these words and expressions from the listening. In your own words, explain what each of them means in the context of the discussion.

1 a male-dominated industry
2 a subtle influence
3 counter-productive efforts
4 the odd woman
5 a token girl fighter
6 secluded market
7 lifeskills
8 to target
9 a successful formula
10 an honorary man

WRITING 1
Reports

1 In Paper 2 you may be asked to write a report. This will usually involve imagining yourself in a situation. Look at this example:

You are working for a company which makes computer games. The company is planning to introduce a new range of games that will appeal especially to young women. Write a report for the company recommending the type of game that should be produced and how this might be marketed.

(about 300 words)

1 Using information from the listening text, plus your personal knowledge of the market for computer games in your own country, make notes under these headings.

The type of games on the market at the moment.
The attitude of young women to computer games.
The type of product your company should develop.
How the product should be marketed and advertised.

2 Compare your notes with your partner. Add any good ideas that your partner has to your notes.

3 How should a report be laid out? Think about:

- Who will read it?
- Why they will read it?
- When and how it might be used?
- What the information will be used for?

4 What style are reports usually written in? Why?
What language forms would you expect to find in a report? Why?
Think about:

- how information is presented
- how opinions are presented

5 Now use your notes to write your report.

READING 1 ▮▮▮
Comprehension

■■ **1** You are going to read an article in which a man talks about the relationships between people in the laboratory where he works. Nine sentences or phrases have been removed from the article. Read carefully and decide which of the sentences or phrases **A–I**, fits in each of the blanks **1–9**.

A But not all lab coats are identical
B But the hierarchy of the coat doesn't end there
C but with a certain difference in the cut
D my clothes are too poor to be troubled by pollution
E protective coats come in several colours
F take it off only to go to the refectory for lunch
G the fact that I'm wearing it at all means that today is a lab day
H the more senior the technician, the less likely to wear a lab coat
I the white coat singles me out

Lab coats

Most days, depending on the trains, I get in about nine o'clock. I dump my coat and bag in the office, pull on a white coat and head for the laboratory. The white coat is important; it has a strong symbolic value. First, **(1)** _____, I'm running an experiment, not to be disrupted with meetings and administrative queries. Second, **(2)** _____, separates me from the rest of the world of non-researchers, who wear no coats. It begins to envelop me in the aura of being a scientist, ready to perform mysterious – almost priestly – labours.

(3) _____, there is a subtle hierarchy amongst them in which their primary function – to keep chemical and biological goo from polluting one's day clothes – has become overladen with symbolism. You don't have to be long in the lab to notice it. First,
10 **(4)** _____; if you're a workshop technician, the coat is likely to be blue, if a porter brown. There's no real reason why a researcher shouldn't wear a blue or brown coat, but the colour difference, like an army uniform is an unspoken indication of rank. If you are lab technician, you'll wear a white coat too, **(5)** _____ – it will button differently at the neck. What's more, you'll be likely to keep it properly fastened at the front. We researchers, on the other hand, leave ours more casually open, swinging around us as we sprint down the corridor from office to lab, though the tradition is fading a bit now as biologists spend less and less time amongst chemical reagents and living things and more in the computer room watching complex multicoloured displays on screens.

(6) _____ . Even if they are given them free, graduate students won't wear lab
20 coats unless they are actually doing something rather hazardous – handling radioactivity, say, when the regulations get quite severe, or a bit bloody, like a minor piece of dissection. The jeans, open collars or tee-shirts that the students wear may also be saying: **(7)** _____ and anyhow I don't want to be fenced in by regulations. At the other end of the hierarchy the rules shift again; **(8)** _____ . Here the message is that I have graduated from lab to office, away from the manual towards mental labour.

Not true for the senior researchers; many who have not been near the lab in years nonetheless put on a spotless white coat each morning as they arrive, sit behind their office desk in it, **(9)** _____ and when they leave for home at 5.30. They'll even go to committee meetings in their lab coats. Again the message is pretty clear: I would like to
30 be down in the lab actually doing experiments with all you guys, I'm just too busy at the moment with a paper, a grant, a committee; but I haven't lost touch with what really matters, and I can still make a scientific contribution, not just an administrative one.

2 The article describes a hierarchy. Complete the grid with information about this hierarchy.

Position in hierarchy	Type of person	Type of coat worn	Their attitude towards the coat

3 Now read the article again and answer these questions.

1 Which verb in paragraph one means 'arrive at work'?

2 What impression is given by the use of the word 'dump'? (line 1)

3 Which verb in paragraph one means 'go towards'?

4 In your own words, explain the meaning of the phrase 'envelop me in the aura'. (lines 5–6)

5 Why has the writer chosen the word 'priestly' in line 6 to describe the scientists work?

6 Which word in paragraph two means 'a dirty substance'?

7 What impression does the writer give by using the word 'sprint' in line 16?

8 Which word in paragraph three is used to mean 'for example?

9 Which word in paragraph three means 'restricted'?

10 In what way have some scientists 'graduated'? (line 25)

11 Which word in the last paragraph means 'clean'?

12 What does the phrase 'what really matters' in lines 31–32 refer to?

SPEAKING 2
Expressing opinions

1 The article talks about symbols of hierarchies. Discuss these questions with your partner.

1 In what other situations are symbols important?

2 What hierarchies do you see around you?

3 Talk about the following areas and the status symbols related to them. Think about:

- rich/poor people
- young/old people
- students/employees
- work/leisure

in relation to:

houses	cars	clothes	hobbies	sports
food and drink		consumer durables		

2 Look at the three photographs. Talk about the people in them in terms of:

- where they stand in a hierarchy;
- where they stand in relation to the people around them;
- how you think they feel about their situation.

SPEAKING 3
Talking about a passage

Read each of these passages quietly to yourself and then talk about them with your partner. Say where you think you might find them, and comment on the language used.

Passage 1

At times when we are unable to run the published timetable because of major problems, such as a long spell of bad weather, major engineering works or problems outside our control, we may introduce an emergency timetable. We aim to give you 24 hours notice of this. Where advance warning is given, the Passenger's Charter and track Record punctuality and reliability performance will be measured against the emergency timetable for the period in question, rather than the normal timetable.

Passage 2

James Dallon was inflating a tractor tyre in the yard when a man he didn't know got out of a blue van and asked if this was the Dallon's house. The man said something about having called in for the raspberries and the last of the peas at James's aunt's house, but James didn't know what he was talking about. The man said he had a message. He didn't smile. James brought him into the kitchen.

USE OF ENGLISH 1
Idioms

1 Look at these idiomatic phrases. What do they have in common?

a keep to the straight and narrow
b take a short cut
c step out of line
d follow in someone's footsteps
e toe the party line
f he didn't put a foot wrong

Now match each of the expressions **a–f** to one of the definitions **1–6**.

1 follow official policy
2 find a quicker way
3 don't deviate from the norm
4 repeat another's experience
5 mistakes were avoided
6 do something unacceptable

2 Fill each of the numbered spaces in the passage with **one** suitable word. The first has been done for you as an example.

Strolling by numbers

Public parks might be more user-friendly if planners (**0**) *took* a mathematical look at their designs. A team of researchers has shown that when left to their (**1**) _____ devices, pedestrians forge complex patterns of paths.

The team were intrigued (**2**) _____ the fact that in many grassy urban parks, the trails left by walkers do not usually mirror the direct routes (**3**) _____ entry and exit points. So, they set (**4**) _____ to predict how the trails in a new park would evolve as pedestrians (**5**) _____ for their favourite routes.

There are several factors (**6**) _____ influence their choices. People usually want to take a direct route to their destination, but they also (**7**) _____ walking on worn trails to trampling over rougher ground. In other (**8**) _____ , it's more convenient to take existing trails than to create new ones. Also, the closer a segment of an existing trail is to a walker, the (**9**) _____ appealing it would seem.

Using these assumptions, the team came (**10**) _____ with four simple equations that describe how the route taken by pedestrians in a flat grassy park would change as time (**11**) _____ . To illustrate the results, they ran a computer simulation in which they opened a square park with a gate at (**12**) _____ corner to a crowd of virtual pedestrians. Each pedestrian had a fixed starting (**13**) _____ and destination, and started at a randomly chosen time.

At (**14**) _____ , when the land was uniformly green with no worn trails, the pedestrians took the six possible direct routes to their destinations. But because not every route was used by the (**15**) _____ number of people, some paths started to (**16**) _____ clearer than others.

As later walkers started to gravitate (**17**) _____ the well-trodden routes, the trails started to bunch (**18**) _____ especially at intersection points, eventually leaving a circuit with an island in the centre – a pattern that naturally appears time and (**19**) _____ in city parks. In effect, the path system shortens with use, until the pattern matches the (**20**) _____ compromise for comfort and brevity for the largest number of people.

3 What conclusions about human nature might you make from the results of this research?

Newspaper articles

1 What makes people want to either:

a follow society's conventions?

b rebel against society's conventions?

2 You are going to read an article about people who have dropped out of society in the USA. These people, who describe themselves as 'gutter punks', live on the streets. What do you expect to read about:

- their appearance/clothes?
- their lifestyle/attitudes?
- the reasons for their lifestyle?
- other people's opinion of them?

3 Now read the article and answer the questions that follow.

BOHEMIA HOSTS ALIENATED TRIBE

As evening falls, the tribe gathers by the river to forage for something to eat, drink or smoke. There is safety in numbers. Wearing studded dog collars, their mohawk haircuts dyed orange and green, their lips and nipples pierced, the tribe lives on the streets, rejecting mainstream America as inane, materialistic and hypocritical.

10 They call themselves 'gutter punks', and they are a new kind of homeless person: white, middle class, often bright, politically militant and homeless by choice. Few are older than 21. Their appearance and their lifestyle may seem a nightmare to their parents and much of society, as if all the promise of youth in America had been turned inside out, producing nihilistic, angry ironic spawn dressed in black – the
20 result of decades of family disintegration, suburban boredom and cynicism.

America has always had its rebels, but where hippies espoused peace, love and a return to the land, today's punks are different. Their world is dark, urban and dangerous. Many drink and do drugs not to have visions, but to black out. 'I only live for three reasons,' says Eric, aged 20, stumbling around the French quarter of
30 New Orleans. 'To drink, to fight and to screw. I'm an escape artist.'

Yet earlier on Hippie Hill that looks out on the quarter's picturesque Jackson Square, Becca, aged 18, who is sober, sweet-faced and carrying a sleepy puppy said: 'People are afraid of us, but we're not the ones who are scary.'

'Tribe' is a word many of them use to describe their sub-culture, complete with
40 ritualistic piercing, tattooing and adornment. New Orleans, a winter haven, probably has thousands in the street at any one time. 'But numbers are really hard to guess', says Paul Rigsby, a private detective who tracks runaways. 'These kids are as migratory as Canada geese'.

New Orleans has everything that punks want: abandoned buildings to squat in, a Bohemian atmosphere and
50 opportunities to pick up food and drink in the street. The number of punks in New Orleans has grown so large that traders and politicians in the French quarter have begun to complain about public urination, drunkenness and fights. Traders circulated a picture of punks entitled: 'Don't feed the animals'. The punks say they are hassled by the police all the time. Homelessness campaigners say the punks are often
60 'swept' from the streets before big local events.

1 Underline all the words used to describe the punks.

2 Underline the parts of the passage where the punks talk about themselves.

3 Underline the parts of the passage where the writer gives his explanation of why the punks behave as they do.

4 Underline the parts of the passage where we hear other people's opinion of the punks.

5 What style is the article written in? Who do you think is the intended audience?

6 How would the article have been different if it had been written for:
   • young people?
   • local people?
   • people who want to help the punks?

7 Using information from the article, but in your own words and in an appropriate style, write either:

   a An article for a local newspaper complaining about the punks and suggesting what should be done about the problem.

   b An article for a young people's magazine that describes the life of the punks in a more positive way.

   c An article for a serious magazine read by people who want to understand and help solve such social problems.

▬ 4 Look at these two extracts taken from a magazine article and talk about:
   • the probable topic of the article
   • the type of magazine it was probably published in
   • the style of the article
   • your opinions about what the people are saying

Fiona from Scotland says:

❝ Those who avert their eyes from the correspondence of others are missing out on one of life's great pleasures. I found a pile on the street once and relished every word. I don't have any qualms about it, actually, and I've become adept at reading upside down, which is useful in cafés and on public transport. It's irresistible, even if it's only a boring letter from the Electricity Company,
10 the fact that it's someone else's is enough, although I'd love to discover people's secrets too, of course. I've never been caught and I'm not remotely ashamed because it's my compulsion. I long for people to read mine, actually, but they never do. ❞

Lawrence from Nigeria says:

❝ I'm against this kind of invasion of privacy because I've been a victim of it. My Mum read a page of mine once and I was livid. My girlfriend has asked about it sometimes, but I think that she realizes that for me this is really a strict no-go area, because it's not really intended for anyone but myself. The last time I looked at someone else's was when I was fourteen and
10 I still feel guilty. I've been curious since, but I've never given in to temptation. Whether or not I found something of interest, I don't think I'd ever do it now because I'd feel shabby, as if I'd betrayed that person's trust. It would be morally wrong. ❞

LISTENING 2
Sentence completion

1 You are going to hear part of a radio discussion on the subject of scientific deception. Before you listen, look at the list of words and phrases in the box. These are from the listening. Use them to discuss these questions.

- What do you think scientific deception is?

- What types of activity do you think it includes?

- What problems do you think might be associated with scientific deception and its discovery and investigation?

deceit	fiddling	fraud	misconduct
proof	reputation	trust	falsify
to point the finger	to blow the whistle	cutting corners	sloppiness
an honest mistake	to turn a blind eye		

2 You will hear part of a radio discussion on the subject of scientific deception. For questions **1–10**, complete the sentences with a word or short phrase.

> ### Scientific deception
>
> Derek says that tackling scientific deception is made more difficult by the absence of a _____ **1** .
>
> Derek describes a mild form of scientific deception as _____ **2** .
>
> The most common form of scientific deception involves the publication of research which has been _____ **3** .
>
> It is less common for scientific data to be _____ **4** .
>
> Heather explains that most successful science involves an element of _____ **5** .
>
> Heather feels that _____ **6** plays a very important role in science.
>
> 'Whistle-blowers' often find themselves accusing their _____ **7** .
>
> It's important that those exposing scientific deception have what Derek calls _____ **8** .
>
> In most cases it is difficult to prove that there is what's termed _____ **9** deceive.
>
> Derek and Heather advocate the setting up of _____ **10** to look into the problem.

3 What do you think about the problem of scientific deception? Look at these comments different people have made about the problem and say to what extent you agree with them.

it's a scandal that should be exposed publicly

it's not a problem as long as it does no harm to anyone

it's not fair to blame individuals if everyone's doing it

it's an inevitable result of human nature

it's a serious crime which should be punished severely

I'm sure there are much worse things going on that we don't know about

GRAMMAR 1

1 What is the difference between deceit and deception? What are the adjectives and adverbs formed from each word?

2 Complete each of these sentences with a verb, noun, adjective or adverb formed from the base word *to deceive*.

1 The puzzle looked _____ easy, but proved very difficult to solve.

2 I don't really trust Lucy, I think she's a really _____ person.

3 That young scientist is not as naive as he seems, you know, appearances can be _____ .

4 I'm afraid Polly is only _____ herself if she thinks her work looks original.

5 It's the quickness of the hand that _____ the eye.

PHRASAL VERBS 1

1 Look at this sentence from the listening. Underline the phrasal verb.

Young scientists are often the ones who come across these things.

2 Complete each sentence with a suitable preposition.

1 John burst _____ the room and told everybody what he had discovered.

2 In the course of the investigation, the scientists came up _____ a number of problems.

3 Whistle-blowers cannot necessarily count _____ the support of their colleagues.

4 It's unlikely that anyone would get _____ with copying whole pieces of someone else's work.

5 A committee is being set _____ to look _____ the whole area of scientific deception.

6 His story was very convincing to the layman, but other scientists saw _____ it immediately.

7 The team came _____ with four simple equations to illustrate their point.

8 The researchers set _____ to predict how trails in a new park would work.

HELP WITH USE OF ENGLISH: GAP-FILL SENTENCES ■■■■■■■■■

In Question 3 of the Use of English paper you have to complete a sentence from which a number of words have been taken out. There may be just one word missing, or there may be as many as five.

Example 1:
The young scientist realized that his boss was falsifying the data, but for fear of losing his job he decided to turn a *blind* eye.

In this example, you have to complete the fixed expression, *to turn a blind eye*. But, sometimes you may have to complete a grammatical form.

Example 2:
As *long as* you warn me in advance, I don't mind you're being late for dinner.

■**1** For questions **1–10**, complete the sentences with a word or phrase from the box.

as it may	bothered one way	but not least	draw the line
far from being	had no choice	it a day	out of the
should have known	the least bit		

1 As night fell on their long search, they decided to give up and call _____ .

2 I can tolerate all kinds of behaviour, but _____ at dishonesty.

3 I _____ better than to leave my private notebook out where David could see it.

4 Strange _____ seem, nobody had thought of reporting the theft of the money to the police.

5 It makes no difference to her; she isn't _____ or the other.

6 As the last bus had already left, we _____ but to order a taxi.

7 _____ disappointed, John seemed quite pleased to have lost the race.

8 And to complete the team, last _____ we have William Webster from London.

9 Despite having made a serious error in her work, Melanie didn't seem _____ embarrassed.

10 I'm afraid that since my horseriding accident, skiing holidays are _____ question.

■**2** For questions **1–5**, complete the expressions with a suitable word or phrase. All the expressions come from this unit or previous units of the book.

1 Instead of walking all the way round the school, Mary took _____ cut through the headmaster's garden.

2 They don't like people with opinions in that organization, they expect you to _____ party line.

3 Joanna decided to be courageous and blow _____ her colleague's dishonesty.

4 Many of the computer games feature the rescue of a damsel _____ .

5 It is generally the man who _____ the day in a difficult situation.

EXAM PRACTICE 8

1 In this section, you must choose the word **A**, **B**, **C** or **D** which best completes each sentence.

1 Advertising a new product is a very costly _____ .

  A concern   **B** affair   **C** pursuit   **D** subject

2 If left to their own _____ , pedestrians make complex patterns of paths.

  A desires   **B** defences   **C** devices   **D** decisions

3 On his way to school, Paul often _____ a short cut across the park.

  A made   **B** took   **C** had   **D** did

4 In exposing the scandal, John was careful not to _____ the finger at his boss.

  A plot   **B** put   **C** place   **D** point

5 Watson said that risk _____ is an important part of science.

  A forming   **B** facing   **C** taking   **D** making

6 As a result of the scandal, the professor suffered a _____ to his reputation.

  A thud   **B** dip   **C** thump   **D** dent

7 When working in the library, I came _____ some very disturbing information.

  A across   **B** against   **C** amongst   **D** amidst

8 Most accusations of scientific deception are strongly _____ .

  A disproved   **B** denied   **C** disagreed   **D** declined

9 If you want to _____ in with gutter punks, you have to look the part.

  A match   **B** melt   **C** fit   **D** set

10 The makers of the popular children's games have found a very _____ market.

  A lucrative   **B** consummate   **C** exhaustive   **D** bountiful

2 Fill each of the numbered blanks in the passage with **one** suitable word.

Action repeat

What in Britain is called *Action Man* was invented in the early sixties in the USA. In order to compensate for perceived prejudice towards the idea of a boy's doll, *GI Joe*, (**1**) _____ the toy is known in America, was made absurdly macho. (**2**) _____ brooding figure, he was muscle-bound, unsmiling, with an ugly scar on (**3**) _____ cheek and hands permanently ready to grab a weapon.

When he came to Britain in 1966, the country was (**4**) _____ quite as obeisant to all things American as it is now. *GI Joe* was translated (**5**) _____ *Action man*, and the outfits reflected Britain's rather (**6**) _____ America's military traditions. These outfits, bought separately from the figure, (**7**) _____ the piece of marketing that (**8**) _____ *Action Man* a cast-iron financial winner. Targeting a small boy's need to collect, the toy offered 350 accessories at its (**9**) _____ in the mid-Seventies, allowing him to build armouries of gleaming hardware.

Action Man (**10**) _____ the 'Toy of the Decade Award' for the Seventies, when it was estimated that children in the UK owned an average of 1.3 *Action Men* (**11**) _____ head. Then, in 1984, the very concept (**12**) _____ deemed too old-fashioned to compete (**13**) _____ computer games, and he was withdrawn (**14**) _____ active service. Thousands of fans, however, continued to collect him and his outfits; (**15**) _____ for annual conventions and pored over each (**16**) _____ displays with relish.

(**17**) _____ 1993, however, the toy company had come to appreciated the power of parental nostalgia in the purchase of children's toys. The lads who had (**18**) _____ up with *Action Man* were happier (**19**) _____ their offspring to play with him than waste their lives in front of screens. So, back he (**20**) _____ , with remodelled hands and new nylon hair, but with the scar intact.

3 Fill each of the blanks with a suitable word or phrase.

1 If you see anything suspicious, the best thing is to _____ eye and say nothing.

2 Harry intends to _____ footsteps and become a partner in the family business.

3 It was a perfect performance by the marathon runner who didn't put _____ wrong during the whole race.

4 Discipline in the army is strict with harsh penalties for anyone who steps _____ line.

5 He took the risk of changing the data knowing that there was a good chance he would _____ with it.

4 For each of the sentences below, write a new sentence as similar as possible in meaning to the original sentence, but using the word given. This word **must not be altered** in any way.

Example: A lot of people attended the meeting.

turnout

Answer: *There was a very poor turnout for the meeting.*

1 The professor wants to show that he is still in touch with his colleagues.

lost

_____

2 Manufacturers may advertise to inform us about their products.

give

_____

3 Maurice was completely unaware that the data was unreliable.

idea

_____

4 After discovering the theft, the only option open to us was calling the police.

but

_____

5 The problem has been caused by sloppiness in research procedures.

resulted

_____

6 How likely is anyone to find out what we have done?

chances

_____

7 That old suede coat no longer looks as good as it once did.

days

_____

8 Tom was not told about the nature of the work the department was engaged in.

dark

_____

9 Ellie was forced to accept a lower position in the company.

choice

_____

10 Phil said to us, 'Please don't tell anyone about my plans to go to New Orleans'.

pleaded

_____

5 Finish each of the following sentences in such a way that it is as similar as possible in meaning to the sentence printed before it.

Example: Immediately after his departure things improved.

Answer: No sooner *had he departed than things improved.*

1 The dentist said Sandra needed to have two fillings.
The dentist said it _____

2 Simon answered the police officer's questions as accurately as he could.
Simon gave _____

3 Tim can't go to the shopping centre without meeting old friends from school.
Whenever _____

4 I'm not angry with you at all Milly, I actually find the situation quite amusing.
Far _____

5 It came as a great surprise to Beryl to find her boss was falsifying his data.
Little _____

6 The scientist never actually claimed that his discovery was a breakthrough.
At no _____

7 Diane thinks that increased use of computers is to blame for falling administrative standards.
Diane puts _____

8 Joan's complaints about her boss were ignored.
Nobody took _____

9 Terry knows is almost completely ignorant when it comes to astronomy.
Terry knows next _____

10 Very few people can claim to have seen a UFO.
Hardly _____

Nose to the Grindstone

Part One
Talking about photographs

1   Look at the four pictures of people working and for each one talk about:

   - the skills required for the job

   - the financial rewards

   - the job satisfaction

   - the advantages and disadvantages

2   How important are the following factors when choosing a career?

   money   job security
   convenience   challenge
   prospects   social aspects
   variety   status
   opportunities for travel, training, creativity, etc.

Part Two
Talking about a passage

1   Read these four passages.

1   Now discuss each one with your partner. Talk about:

- where you might find it
- its purpose
- the style and register
- the intended audience
- your reaction to it

2   Look at passages 1 and 3. They are both job advertisements which were placed in a scientific magazine by large companies. Compare and contrast them in terms of:

- the style of writing
- the use of language
- their effect on the reader

Passage 1

> The post of
> # Operations Engineer
> has been created following the restructuring of the department.

The post requires excellent management ability coupled with a high level of scientific competence.

Applicants must have a minimum of four year's experience as a B grade clinical scientist and have a solid background in electronic engineering, together with substantial experience of equipment management and development.

Applicants must have a first degree in a relevant scientific subject and preferably a higher degree or management qualification.

Essential personal qualities are self-motivation, commitment to working as part of a team and the ability to communicate well with other staff at all levels.

Passage 2

It had to happen!

Our continuing growth (thank you!) means we've at last had to bow to the inevitable and install a computer system.

Even as we write we're up to our ears in RAMS and ROMS and bits and bytes. The system will 'go live' in late Summer/early Autumn and a few teething troubles are always a possibility. So, please bear with us and don't hesitate to call if you experience any problems. As the saying goes, 'To err is human, but to really foul things up requires a computer'. Hopefully, we will fairly quickly be able to start providing you with the improved level of service which is the whole point of putting in the computer in the first place!

Passage 3

As a formulation chemist, you'll be right at the heart of the things we do here, working with equally able people from many different disciplines and with the latest lab equipment at your disposal.

You will apply chemistry to the design and preparation of samples and use a range of techniques to analyze them. It's work that will use and build on the knowledge you gained in your degree course and it will test and develop your ability to work with people and to respond to their great ideas as well as developing your own.

Finally, if you prefer acres of green instead of tonnes of concrete, you'll feel totally at home working with us in Berkshire.

Please apply in writing with a full CV and covering letter.

Passage 4

People often tell us we're the friendliest, most helpful phone people in the business. And without meaning to sound boastful, we think it's true.

Our operators are trained to know our products inside out; they have detailed specs of everything we sell at their fingertips and can give you the complete run down on all our services. And rest assured, we're happy for them to spend as much time with you as necessary to answer any questions you might have and help make your shopping experience a real pleasure.

Part Three
Discussing a task

1 What makes a good employee? Make a list of the personal qualities you would look for if you were employing someone.

2 What is the best way to recruit staff? Talk about the advantages and disadvantages of each of the following as a way of selecting people:
- application form
- references
- interview
- trial period
- personality test
- personal recommendation

USE OF ENGLISH 1
Cloze passage

■ **1** Fill each of the numbered spaces in the passage with **one** suitable word. The first one has been done for you as an example.

When Caruso met Puccini

The story of how Enrico Caruso, the great operatic tenor first met composer Giacomo Puccini (**0**) _could_ easily have come from a Hollywood musical, if (**1**) _____ from opera itself.

Imagine (**2**) _____ scene. A young man and woman are in love. She is to star in a show; he wishes to play opposite her, (**3**) _____ he is unknown. She challenges (**4**) _____ to audition before the composer himself; he accepts, overrides all obstacles of protocol, and performs with (**5**) _____ stunning artistry and style that the (**6**) _____ is instantly his.

Unfortunately, our lover did not quite (**7**) _____ the part. He was short and tubby, with an undistinguished moustache and an undesirable accent. It was the composer (**8**) _____ was handsome and debonair.

What our lover (**9**) _____ have, however, was the optimism of youth. With all the engaging audacity (**10**) _____ a film hero, Enrico Caruso, wanting very (**11**) _____ to sing Rudolfo in *La Boheme*, (**12**) _____ unannounced one day in June 1897, at the Tuscan home of Giacomo Puccini.

He was admitted (**13**) _____ protest. Puccini, a wide brimmed hat on his head, ushered him (**14**) _____ a studio made stifling (**15**) _____ a roaring fire. Perspiring (**16**) _____ heat and nervousness, Caruso asked to sing from the opera. Puccini obligingly sat down (**17**) _____ the piano. It (**18**) _____ only a few bars for the composer to realize (**19**) _____ in tone and dramatic intensity here was the perfect, the ultimate, Rudolfo. With the final note, Puccini spun (**20**) _____ in genuine amazement. 'Who has sent you to me' he asked, 'God?'

■ **2** Find words in the passage that mean:

   a official or accepted procedure
   b best area
   c extremely impressive
   d rather overweight
   e trial performance by an applicant for a job in the performing arts
   f well mannered
   g daring
   h hot and airless
   i sweating

WRITING 1
Formal letters 1

1 Imagine you have to interview someone for each of the jobs advertised below. With your partner draw up a list of questions you would want to ask each person applying for each of the jobs.

> We are looking for a reliable person to look after William (aged 3) and Sophie (aged 2). Only experienced nannies or au pairs with good references need apply. We provide clean accommodation, full board, plus every Sunday off. Competitive salary. We are based in London and would offer a 4-month contract to the right person; renewable by mutual consent.
>
> Please apply in writing, giving full personal details and enclosing a photograph to:
>
> *Mr & Mrs Sloane, P.O. Box 251, London W1*

> **Are you: patient flexible? responsible? reliable? good in a crisis? and fun?**
>
> If so, you could be the type of person we are looking for. We need someone to spend time with Paul (8), Samantha (11) and Jason (13) over the summer holidays. They like computers, animals and mountain bikes. We like peace and quiet. Full board provided, plus some time off. Rural location. If you think this sounds like you, write telling us all about yourself to:
>
> **Simon & Kate Freeman, Forest Cottage, near Mowtown, England.**

2 Imagine that you are interested in applying for one of these two jobs.

Write a letter to the employer in which you:
- introduce yourself
- say why you think you would be suitable
- ask for more information about the job

You may write about your real self or invent the information if you prefer.

3 Before you write anything, talk to your partner and make notes. Think about:
- the information you should include (e.g. family background, education, experience, hobbies, personality, etc.)
- the order in which things are presented
- the layout and organization of the letter
- the appropriate style for the letter

4 Use your notes to plan your letter. Then write it.

Multiple choice

1 Discuss these points with your partner.

1 What are the advantages and
disadvantages of:

- working mothers
- nannies
- nursery schools

2 Read the article about nannies.

DOES MUMMY KNOW BEST?

FOR WORKING WOMEN, entrusting children to a stranger is often a necessity. But, the subject of nannies, like hunting, is guaranteed to turn the most mild-mannered person into a ranting omniscient fiend.

When I first hired a nanny, three years ago, half my friends were appalled. What is the point of having children, they said, if you're not prepared to look after them? They cited
10 Sigmund Freud's widely accepted theory about the first five years of life being the ones that determine behaviour throughout life. Was I really willing to leave this most onerous of tasks to a stranger? Was I prepared for the hideous eventuality of having my son love his nanny more than he did me?

The other half, old nanny hands themselves, whooped for joy. I had seen the light, they said. I would now be fulfilled by my work as
20 well as by my child, and would as a result be a better mother. You need adult company sometimes, they said, and intellectual stimulation. Children are lovely, but lovelier still if you have the odd break from them. They'll always love you more, because you are their mother – thinking otherwise is simply paranoia. And you need to earn your own money to keep your self respect. What do you want to be – a housewife? Pull the other one.

30 Judge not, lest you be judged. The first rule of parenting is not to cast aspersions on the way other people bring up their children. But with the best will in the world it is hard to watch *Quality Time*, a documentary about working mothers, nannies and children to be screened on *BBC2* next week, without getting angry. It isn't that all three women – Janis, who works in public relations, Caroline, a beauty PR, and Dominique, a clothing executive – employ nannies. Nannies, after all, are a fact of life for many working women.

40 What is so shocking, in a programme that will surely go down as one of the great TV stitch-ups, is the women's apparent disregard for their children's emotional well-being. One gets the impression that not one of them knows her child, or even wants to. 'I'm not used to children,' deadpans one of the mothers. 'After all, I've only had them for five years.' And if that little admission doesn't make your jaw drop, I don't know what will.

Dominique has two nannies on duty 24 hours a day,
50 one for each little daughter. And a weekend nanny too, of course. And a holiday nanny. According to one nanny, Dominique has never – not once – got up in the night to comfort her crying child. You get the picture? Her daughters do: they see their mother so little that they take her photograph to bed with them to talk to.

Heartbroken sobbing permeates the programme, as almost all of the children featured learn that their beloved nanny – the one who plays, kisses,
60 comforts, gets up in the night – has gone away for a long 'holiday'. Again. 'So far we've had sixteen nannies,' says Caroline's five year old daughter. Actually it has only been six, but out of the mouths of babes…

What's so grotesquely compelling about the documentary is the casual, systematic way that all three children – outwardly privileged – are emotionally bludgeoned before our eyes. They evidently have only a minimal attachment to their absentee mothers: that privilege is reserved for their nannies. And the nannies keep disappearing. No one explains why, so the bewildered children just cry, harder each time, as any sense of security they might once have enjoyed becomes ever more eroded.

That this will result in emotionally damaged children would be blindingly obvious to an amoeba – but not, apparently, to this trio of mothers in their power suits. But what if this style of parenting isn't bad, just honest? Should we admire Caroline for admitting she's 'not very good with children' despite having two of her own? 'I was getting on', she says in the film, 'I thought I might as well have them'. When I speak to her later she says, 'I had them very late. I'm a career woman!'

It is, conceivably, brave to identify your weak spot – children – and let others take care of it, while you concentrate on what you are good at: work. Of her weak spot, Caroline says, 'I know I wouldn't be much fun with them all day every day. I'm not motherly in that way.' Janis meanwhile, sees nothing amiss in her two-year old daughter having had six nannies, including a maternity nurse. 'Because she has been looked after by so many people, she is very independent,' says Janis, 'On her first day at school, she just breezed in'. Caroline agrees. 'The girls are amazingly unfazed by the succession of nannies. They know we are coming home at the end of the day.'

I suggest that it must be nice for the girls to know that their mother will be there to give them breakfast and put them to bed. 'Actually, the nanny gives them breakfast – I'm busy getting ready,' is the reply. 'Sometimes I don't see them at all in the mornings. It doesn't bother me or the girls'.

Since I have given the three women featured in *Quality Time* a hard time, perhaps I should give them a chance to do it to me. I packed my job in – and the £50,000 a year that went with it – to become a housewife. Because I believe that little children need their mothers. And the best nanny in the world is no substitute for the worst mother. Basically, I think that if you have children you should look after them.

3 Now answer the questions **1–6**. Choose the answer **A**, **B**, **C** or **D** which you think fits best.

1 When the writer first employed a nanny
A most of her friends disapproved.
B some of her friends deserted her.
C none of her friends were surprised.
D all of her friends reacted strongly.

2 In the writer's opinion, parents should not
A criticise the lifestyle of other families.
B entrust our children to strangers.
C take the programme too seriously.
D get angry at the three women.

3 What does the writer feel most strongly about with regard to the TV programme?
A The TV company's attitude to the women.
B The women's attitude to their children.
C The level of responsibility given to nannies.
D The intrusion of the programme into private affairs.

4 What causes most problems for the children seen in the film?
A inconsistent discipline
B turnover of staff
C lack of affection
D poorly trained nannies

5 How do the children's mothers feel about the situation?
A They try to justify their decisions.
B They refuse to accept any criticisms.
C They are aware of the problems.
D They blame their staff for any difficulties.

6 How can we best summarize the writer's general attitude towards working mothers?
A fairly critical
B rather sceptical
C relatively understanding
D largely unimpressed

4 Find these expressions in the article. In your own words, explain what the writer means by each of them. (paragraph numbers in brackets)

1 old nanny hands (3)
2 pull the other one (3)
3 to cast aspersions (4)
4 the best will in the world (4)
5 make your jaw drop (5)
6 you get the picture (6)
7 outwardly privileged (8)
8 getting on (9)
9 sees nothing amiss (10)
10 breezed in (10)
11 unfazed (10)
12 packed in (12)

5 Discuss these questions with your partner.

● Do you have any sympathy with the women in the programme?
● In what way might the programme have been unfair?
● What style of writing has the writer adopted? Why?
● Where would you expect to find this article?
● What type of person would read it?
● Would they agree with it?

WRITING 2
Formal letters 2

1 Write one of the following letters to the journalist.

a A letter from one of the mothers defending yourself and complaining about how the programme was made.

b A letter from a working mother or a nanny pointing out that not all children with working mothers suffer in the ways described in the article.

c A letter from somebody who agrees with the points made in the article, quoting personal experience.

SPEAKING 2
Discussing proverbs

1 Look at these two proverbs which the writer quotes in the article.

judge not lest you be judged
out of the mouths of babes ...

Why did the writer choose to use these expressions?

2 Look at these proverbs and sayings and discuss the extent to which they reflect truths about the society in which we live. Do they have equivalents in your language?

a one man's meat is another man's poison
b like father like son
c clothes maketh the man
d pride comes before a fall
e many a true word is said in jest
f people who live in glass houses shouldn't throw stones

Nouns formed from phrasal verbs

1

1 Look at this phrase from the article.

The programme will surely go down as one of the great TV stitch-ups.

2 What is a stitch-up?

This compound noun is formed from the phrasal verb *to stitch (someone) up*. Notice that this noun is hyphenated. Other nouns of this type are single words e.g. *feedback*, although the order of the words may change, e.g. *an outbreak of flu*.

2 Complete each sentence with a noun formed from a phrasal verb. Use the verb in brackets.

1 Police are on the _____ for a man with dark hair and a grey moustache. (look)

2 John apologized for his angry _____ during the discussion. (burst)

3 Mr Smith was delayed as he had a _____ on the motorway. (break)

4 Sally is responsible for cleaning, repairs and the general _____ of the building. (keep)

5 The meeting finished without coming to a satisfactory _____ . (come)

6 Scientists have announced a _____ in their search for a cure for the disease. (break)

7 The company has reported an _____ in its profits this year. (turn)

8 I am not working this evening, but I can't go out because I am on _____ . (stand)

3 Phrasal verbs can also be used to form adjectives. Look at the example.

The <u>breakdown</u> truck moved slowly because it was towing a damaged car.

4 Complete each of these sentences with an adjective formed from a phrasal verb. Use the verb in brackets.

1 Louise looked in the mirror, sighed, and reached for her _____ bag. (make)

2 Mary couldn't be bothered to cook, so she bought a _____ pizza on her way home. (take)

3 Jim found the interviewer's abrupt manner very _____ . (put)

4 Dawn is an _____ tennis player who has won many championships. (stand)

5 Mr Thomas, flying to Miami, is asked to return to the _____ desk where his boarding card is ready for collection. (check)

6 The family business was the subject of a _____ bid by a large multi-national company. (take)

🔲 LISTENING 1
Multiple choice

▬ 1 What do you think are the advantages of a small family-run business:

- for the consumer/clients?
- for the owner?
- for the employees?

▬ 2 You will hear part of a radio programme about a small business involved in tea-blending. For questions **1–5**, choose the alternative **A**, **B**, **C** or **D** which fits best according to what you hear.

1 Mr Miles believes that his teas are popular because

A they are similar to those of larger companies.
B holidaymakers buy them as souvenirs.
C his company is able to maintain high quality.
D his teas are typical of that part of the country.

2 What is Mr Miles' opinion of teabags?

A He would prefer not to sell them.
B The tea in them is of inferior quality.
C Most of his customers prefer loose tea.
D They are not particularly convenient.

3 As Mr Miles' business has grown, what has remained the same?

A the number of people he works with
B the amount of time he spends at work
C the device he uses for measuring the tea
D the types of tea which he produces

4 What does Mr Miles do to ensure the quality of his tea?

A He experiments with different types of tea.
B He spends most of his time tasting tea.
C He adjusts the quantities of different teas used in a blend.
D He uses information passed on by his grandfather.

5 What is Mr Miles' view of the tea industry?

A He'd like to escape from it.
B It's in need of some new ideas.
C It is rather old-fashioned.
D Family ties are overstressed.

▬ 3 Listen again and make a note of the words and phrases that tell us:

- two ways teas are sold
- how quality is maintained
- Mr Miles' attitude to his work

READING 2
Comprehension

1 Before you read the article discuss these questions with your partner.

1 Would you prefer to work for yourself or a company?

2 In choosing a company to work for, which of the following factors would be important to consider?

Box 1

size of company	quality of staff	reputation of company
management structure	quality of product	decision-making process
attitude towards staff	location	business methods
recruitment process	perks	

3 Look at the words in Box 2. What does each of them mean in the context of an employee in a large company?

Box 2

redundancy	cost-cutting	downsizing	efficiency	loyalty
bottom line	competitive	workload	profitability	

2 Look at this headline. What situation do you think the article is going to describe?

Read the article and answer the questions which follow it.

WHO LOVES THE FIRM TODAY?

Downsizing has turned workers into couldn't-care-less cynics. Even the companies are worried.

Downsizing became one of the key business concepts of the 1990s. For some it represented all that was good, efficient and forward-looking, but for others it signalled the end of all they had worked for. Downsizing is defined as the 'energetic pursuit of cost-cutting as a means of survival or a route to greater profitability'. Put simply, a company could make more money if the same amount of work could be done by fewer people. And, of course, in a competitive environment, once one company succeeded in doing it, they all had to jump on the bandwagon or go under. What it meant for many loyal, enthusiastic employees, along with a
10 few dud ones, was that they were suddenly, inexplicably, made redundant.

Exponents of downsizing, however, failed to predict the effects of the process on both the attitude of the staff who held on to their jobs and on the attitudes of the workforce in general. The theory had been that the survivors of downsizing, fearful for their own jobs, would keep their heads down, work harder and cling enthusiastically to the wreckage. If their endurance failed, there would always be plenty of others only too ready to take their place. After all, the theory went, any prospective employee, having previously been sacked, would have learnt a keen respect for a full-time job.

But things have not worked out quite as anticipated. Unexpected outcomes of the cutbacks in white-collar jobs have been outlined in a recent book, *The Loyalty Effect* by Frederick Reichheld. The victims of these layoffs, he argues, can have a tough time regaining their balance. They also carry an important lesson: never, ever to give that kind of blind dedication and loyalty to a company again. Survivors have a tough time too. They have to cope not only with their natural anxiety about future rounds of cuts, they also have to take on the added workload of those who were laid off. And for this increased workload, they see little in the way of increased compensation.

Research has found a great deal of anger among staff who survived the upheavals of the cost-cutting measures. They felt tension between, on the one hand, the desire to hold onto their precious permanent jobs as experienced incumbents, and on the other, the feeling that they should be getting out, making contacts and acquiring skills that might be useful in the future; just in case they should be next on the list. They were the most fearful sector of all and somewhat aggrieved that values of loyalty and employer-related skills were being discounted against the bottom-line.

This view that loyalty is a thing of the past is gaining ground. More and more, the conventional wisdom is that employees must take full responsibility for their own careers and that the key to success is watching out for number one.

The big downside of this new attitude is now being felt by companies. All smart firms realize that healthy profits depend upon loyal customers. And the best way to keep them happy is through loyal employees who treat them well, who are a name and a voice in an otherwise faceless bureaucracy and who can build a long-term relationship with customers.

Company restructuring has thrown this delicate balance into jeopardy. As a result of endless cost-cutting changes, US companies now lose half their customers in five years, half their employees in four, and half their investors in less than one year. The picture is not that different in Europe: Loyalty is becoming a big problem, particularly among younger recruits. Research has found that only 37% of young workers describe themselves as loyal. This has consequences for the business itself. Where there is a massive turnover of personnel, the staff dealing with sales often do not know either the product or the customer. Paperwork is often done in a sloppy way because employees thinking they have no long-term future in the company, have no investment in getting it right. Even more serious, job insecurity accompanied by low wages and broken loyalties means that some employees decide to get the most out of the company while they are there. This leads to company secrets being sold to the highest bidder. The traditional controls which companies put in to stop this, and problems such as fraud, are based on a mutual trust that may no longer be there.

Many companies have been slow to recognize the consequences of their own short-termist cost cutting. Some have begun to move back towards the notion of 'jobs for life' in an attempt to improve staff morale and thence the quality of service to customers. In others, managers are taking time to explain to employees how they could have a career with the company, whilst supervisors do simple things to build a team spirit, like going out for a drink with their staff. This seems like little more than common sense, and it is perhaps a comment on how bad things have become that even these basic measures are now being explained to companies by highly-paid consultants.

1 What were the two main reasons why companies went in for downsizing in the 1990s?

2 Which idiomatic phrase in paragraph one means to do what everybody else is doing?

3 What, according to the writer, was the alternative to downsizing for many companies?

4 In your own words explain why many employees found it 'inexplicable' that they were made redundant.

5 What two factors did companies believe would motivate their employees after downsizing had taken place?

6 What are the two main effects of downsizing on those employees who 'survive' it?

7 What synonyms of redundancy are used in paragraph three?

8 Which word in paragraph four means 'disruptive changes'?

9 Which phrase in paragraph five is used to mean 'becoming more accepted'?

10 Compare the meaning of the word 'key' as used in line 52, with the meaning of the same word as used in the first line of the article.

11 In your own words, explain the meaning of the phrase 'watching out for number one'.

12 Which word in paragraph six is used to mean 'drawback' or 'disadvantage'?

13 What does the writer mean by the phrase 'faceless bureaucracy'? (line 60)

14 What idiomatic phrase in paragraph seven means 'put at risk'?

15 Which phrase from paragraph seven is used to describe the phenomenon of workers joining and leaving companies regularly?

16 Which word in paragraph seven means 'careless'?

17 Who do you think is 'the highest bidder' in line 86?

18 Which crime is mentioned in paragraph seven?

19 In your own words, explain the term 'staff morale'. (line 95)

20 In your own words, explain the term 'team spirit'. (lines 100–101)

21 In a paragraph of 70–90 words, summarize the negative consequences of downsizing that are described in the article.

GRAMMAR 1
Reference skills

1 Look at these words of reference used in the article. For each one, mark the passage to show what is being referred to. The first one has been done for you as an example.

a	it (line 8)	**g**	it (line 81)
b	their place (line 15)	**h**	this (line 85)
c	they (line 24)	**i**	this (line 88)
d	they (line 32)	**j**	others (line 97)
e	them (line 59)	**k**	this (line 102)
f	this (line 73)		

Downsizing is defined as the 'energetic pursuit of cost-cutting as a means of survival or a route to greater profitability'. Put simply, a company could make more money if the same amount of work could be done by fewer people. And, of course, in a competitive environment, once one company succeeded in doing it, they all had to jump on the bandwagon or go under.

2 Who are the 'some' and 'others' referred to in the first paragraph? Why has the writer used these pronouns?

3 Who are the 'some' and 'others' referred to in the final paragraph? Why has the writer used these pronouns on this occasion?

4 What is the function of these phrases in terms of what comes before and after them?

    a put simply (line 6)
    b after all (line 15)
    c just in case (42)
    d more and more (line 49)
    e even more serious (line 81)

WRITING 3
Discursive writing

1 With your partner:

- discuss **one** of the following composition titles;
- make notes of the points you each raise;
- use your notes to plan a composition.

2 Now write your composition. Write no more than 300 words.

    a What should companies do to make sure that, whilst remaining competitive, they retain the loyalty of their employees?

    b What advice would you give a young person just about to start a career in a large multinational company which is known to have a large turnover of staff?

☐ LISTENING 2
Part One
Listening for specific information

1 Have you ever played *Monopoly*?
Tell your partner what you know
about the game. Talk about:

- the idea behind the game
- how you play
- what skills you need to win
- why it is so popular

2 Listen to the beginning
of a radio programme about
Monopoly. Some numbers are
mentioned in the programme.
As you listen, note down what
these numbers refer to.

2 =   36 =
3 =   1935 =
4 =   15,140 =
5 =   1,000,000 =
25 =   160,000,000 =

3 Listen again to check your notes, and then tell your partner how
the tournament is organized.

Part Two

Sentence completion

■■ 1   Now listen to another part of the programme which talks about how *Monopoly* was first introduced to Britain. For questions **1–7**, complete the sentences with a word or short phrase.

Monopoly

In order to assess the game, the chairman of Waddingtons played it with [＿＿＿＿＿ **1**] .

The chairman was so excited that he decided to contact the USA via [＿＿＿＿＿ **2**] .

Parker Brothers agreed to work with Waddingtons because they thought the company [＿＿＿＿＿ **3**] .

In adapting the game for Britain, the chairman sent his [＿＿＿＿＿ **4**] to London.

The streets were chosen according to how familiar they would be to [＿＿＿＿＿ **5**] .

One part of the board was named after a pub called [＿＿＿＿＿ **6**] .

It is now possible to play a version of *Monopoly* [＿＿＿＿＿ **7**] .

■■ 2   Match one phrase on the left with one on the right to complete a common expression used in the listening. The first one has been done for you as an example.

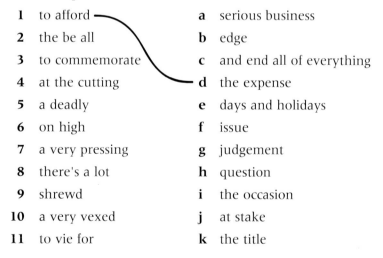

1	to afford	**a**	serious business
2	the be all	**b**	edge
3	to commemorate	**c**	and end all of everything
4	at the cutting	**d**	the expense
5	a deadly	**e**	days and holidays
6	on high	**f**	issue
7	a very pressing	**g**	judgement
8	there's a lot	**h**	question
9	shrewd	**i**	the occasion
10	a very vexed	**j**	at stake
11	to vie for	**k**	the title

■■ 3   Mark the stressed syllable on these words from the listening texts.

monopoly	technology	telephonic	commemorate
championship	regulations	preliminary	property
engineer	competitors	tournament	opponent

Now listen again to check your answers to questions 2 and 3 above.

EXAM PRACTICE 9

1 In this section you must choose the word **A**, **B**, **C** or **D** which best completes each sentence.

1 We hope that within the _____ of a few weeks, we'll have sorted out the backlog of orders.

    A limit   **B** end   **C** space   **D** time

2 The local people _____ Miles Tea as a great luxury.

    A hail   **B** cheer   **C** address   **D** deem

3 Breakfast Blend makes up the _____ of the company's business.

    A bulge   **B** bulk   **C** mass   **D** weight

4 Mr Miles is a traditionalist _____ heart.

    A in   **B** on   **C** to   **D** at

5 Tea bags do not really _____ with his approval.

    A make   **B** meet   **C** count   **D** get

6 We've had to _____ to the inevitable and install a computer.

    A bend   **B** nod   **C** stoop   **D** bow

7 At the moment we're up to our _____ in problems associated with the new system.

    A chins   **B** brows   **C** noses   **D** ears

8 Larger organizations often _____ for national advertising.

    A decide   **B** prefer   **C** choose   **D** opt

9 We won the contract thanks to the _____ judgement of our chairman.

    A shrewd   **B** crafty   **C** smart   **D** cunning

10 It conformed to the way business was normally _____ in those days.

    A conveyed   **B** conducted   **C** carried   **D** comported

2 Fill each of the numbered blanks in the passage with **one** suitable word.

A Sticky Business

The post-it note is that rare thing; a genuine invention. New products constantly appear, but (**1**) _____ all are refinements of earlier versions of the (**2**) _____ idea. In marketing terms, the post-it met an unperceived need because initially no one (**3**) _____ see the point of it.

One Sunday, Arthur Fry (**4**) _____ sang in a choir at his local church, was marking the pages of his hymn book in the time-honoured (**5**) _____ with scraps of paper. (**6**) _____ usually happened, they soon (**7**) _____ out. 'Why', he wondered, 'has no one ever invented a sticky bookmark?' Eureka!

For during the week, Fry worked for the 3M company as a chemist. The following Monday, he dug (**8**) _____ the formula for an unusual adhesive developed by one of his colleagues, Dr Spencer Silver. (**9**) _____ glue had 'low tack', which meant that it stuck (**10**) _____ didn't bond tightly. Its outstanding feature was that it could be peeled off without (**11**) _____ any trace. Until then, (**12**) _____ Dr Silver nor his colleagues had been able to think of a use for

Fry began to experiment. (**13**) _____ many hymn book pages had been glued inseparably together, he came (**14**) _____ with what we would (**15**) _____ as a post-it note. Impressed, 3M (**16**) _____ ahead with test marketing. The first results were rather disappointing. Then someone noticed that (**17**) _____ free samples had been (**18**) _____ out, sales were very good. That observation probably saved the yellow sticker (**19**) _____ obscurity. Post-it notes are now (**20**) _____ the five top-selling 3M products.

3 Fill each of the blanks with a suitable word or phrase.
1 Our salespersons are highly-trained and know our products _____ out.
2 Success in business is a matter of being in the right _____ time.
3 Our telephone operators have the information you need _____ fingertips.
4 Most people only play *Monopoly* on high days and _____.
5 Turn it off now, Bobby; computers aren't the be all _____ everything.

4 For each of the sentences below, write a new sentence as similar as possible in meaning to the original sentence, but using the word given. This word **must not be altered** in any way.

Example: A lot of people attended the meeting.

turnout

Answer: *There was a very good turnout for the meeting.*

1 Please call at once if you have any problems.

hesitate

_____

2 The view that loyalty is a thing of the past is becoming more prevalent.

ground

_____

3 It is extremely important that tea is blended in the right way.

utmost

_____

4 The falling exchange rate threatens to jeopardize our foreign holiday.

thrown

_____

5 Doctors reported that cholera had broken out in remote villages.

outbreak

_____

6 Please wait a moment while I consult the file.

bear

_____

7 The number of customers re-ordering goods from the company has increased.

upturn

_____

8 The post requires a combination of management ability and scientific competence.

coupled

_____

9 As part of its restructuring programme, the company is laying off some employees.

redundant

_____

10 The company has announced that spending on staff training is to be reduced.

cutbacks

_____

5 Finish each of the following sentences in such a way that it means the same as the sentence printed before it.

Example: Immediately after his departure things improved.

Answer: No sooner *had he departed than things improved.*

1 I think about changing my job almost every day.
Hardly _____

2 You will not be made redundant unless you have a poor work record.
As long _____

3 Only those applicants attending the interview will be considered for the job.
Unless _____

4 There are rumours that the company is about to reduce its workforce.
The company is _____

5 If we hope to maintain profitability, there is no alternative but to cut costs.
Only by _____

6 Amongst the steelworkers there was widespread opposition to the new contract.
Most of _____

7 Mr Groves will not hesitate to dismiss you if your work does not improve.
Mr Groves will have _____

8 Although we all expected Toby to apply for the job, he decided not to.
Contrary _____

9 Great fun as speed cycling is, mountain biking manages to be even more so.
Speed cycling doesn't _____

10 For a climber of Ben's skill, the rock face posed no great problem.
For such _____

The Road Ahead

Planning

1 Look at the photographs of people on holiday. With your partner, talk about each of the photographs and say what type of people are attracted to each type of holiday and why.

2 What makes a good tourist resort?

1 You have been asked to design a new tourist resort in your country, or the country where you are studying. Talk to your partner and make notes under these headings:

Where? What? For whom?

- location
- accommodation
- families with children
- setting
- facilities
- young people
- access
- entertainments
- retired people

2 How will you promote the resort? Talk about the effectiveness of:

- advertising in newspapers; magazines; TV & radio
- brochures
- mailshots
- travel agents

3 Imagine that you have to write a leaflet of 150 words to promote your resort.

- What information will it contain?
- What style will it be written in?
- What type of language will it use?
- What visual images will you use?

4 Write the text of your leaflet.

READING 1
Comprehension

1 Discuss these questions with your partner.

1 What things do you associate with:

a tourists?
b backpackers?

Talk about:

| clothes | equipment | destinations |
| means of transport | souvenirs | attitudes to others |

2 Read the article quickly to see how many of the things you talked about are mentioned.

Not the Done Thing: BACKPACKING

Like most nomadic tribes, backpackers have evolved a complex system of appearance and behaviour in order to recognize each other, and – more importantly – to distinguish themselves from their enemies: tourists. So perhaps it is no surprise that to outsiders they all look the same: same packs, same clothes; frequently in possession of the same guidebook. Lesson one if you want to fit in
10 **with backpackers – look the part.**

The accepted backpacker dress code is standard-issue jeans and T-shirts, mixed with ethnic stuff picked up along the road. Brightly-coloured scarves, Baggy Indian trousers, sarongs, odd bits of cut-price jewellery, itself often made by other backpackers. Absolutely prohibited is any kind of practical Western gear designed for travelling lightweight; crease-free clothing, for example, or khaki shirts with many pockets.

When it comes to equipment, no backpacker by
20 definition, would commit social suicide by setting forth with a suitcase. Your pack is a social statement. Do not hang camping equipment from it like a Scout, and definitely do not adorn it with your country's flag.

Backpackers like to think of themselves as citizens of the world, and at home anywhere. They do not like to advertise the fact that their actual homes lie in the suburbs.

You may carry a camera, but use it discreetly, to take snapshots of other backpackers – never
30 of locals, which is something only tourists do. Needless to say, there is no known instance of any backpacker carrying a camcorder.

You must also be discreet in your use of the *Lonely Planet Guide* (or similar). This is an object of tortured ambivalence in the backpacking world. While all backpackers carry one, few draw attention to the fact, and no one ever consults it in public (as a tourist would). And only the truly desperate
40 would attempt to use it as a conversation piece. A lone backpacker reading a *Rough Guide* in a foreign place may as well hang a sign around his neck saying, 'Sad case. Please talk to me.'

As for other reading matter, books by Hermann Hesse and other half-baked mystics –– once required backpacker authors – have gone firmly out of fashion, and will cause your

50 peers to regard you as a nerd. These days any old airport novel will do: the thicker the better.

Backpackers, as is well known, travel to meet locals – provided that the locals are poor, dispossessed or engaged in some colourful profession such as ear-cleaning or rickshaw driving. Backpackers do not talk to members of the professional classes, such as business-persons. These are looked down upon as some sort of honorary tourists in their own country.

60 But the single most important characteristic of the authentic backpacker is an obsession with price. Without this you cannot hope to be accepted into the backpacking community. Transport, food, and accommodation must all be the cheapest possible. Anyone who spends an extra quid on a decent-sized room when there are cheaper ones available; who splurges on a meal in an expensive restaurant, or (heaven forbid) takes a taxi rather than a
70 bus is asking for mockery and eventual social ostracism. He has just identified himself as a tourist.

It is as well to remember this when conversing with backpackers. Like birds, many of them seem to communicate with a limited series of notes. Questions such as 'Where have you been?'
80 and 'How much did it cost?' are the staple of the backpacker's conversation. Digging deeper – by asking such questions as 'Why are you here?' – may be taken as intrusive. Worse, they will lump you in with another category of
90 person regarded by all backpackers as utterly beyond the pale. Second only to 'tourist' in backpacker demonology is, of course, 'parent'.

3   Now read the article again and answer these questions.

1   In your own words, explain how backpackers are like 'nomadic tribes'. (line 1)

2   Which verb in paragraph one means 'to be accepted by'?

3   Which verb in paragraph two means 'acquired'?

4   In your own words, explain what the writer means by the phrase 'commit social suicide'. (line 20)

5   What is the 'social statement' made by a pack in line 21?

6   Why do backpackers not carry camcorders?

7   What is 'ambivalent' about the backpackers attitude to guidebooks?

8   In your own words explain what is meant by the term 'conversation piece'. (lines 40–41)

9   What do you think the verb 'to splurge' means? (line 68)

10   In your own words, explain why a backpacker would not take a taxi.

11   What does the writer mean by the phrase 'digging deeper'? (lines 83–84)

12   Which phrase in the last paragraph means 'totally unacceptable'?

13   Why does the writer say that backpackers are like birds?

14   How would you describe the style of the article? Who do you think is the intended reader?

15   What do the following words from the text refer to?
     a   they (line 7)
     b   itself (line 14)
     c   it (line 22)
     d   they (line 26)
     e   You (line 33)
     f   one (line 37)
     g   your peers (lines 48–49)
     h   this (line 62)

16   In a paragraph of between 70–90 words, summarize the things which, according to the writer, backpackers do to differentiate themselves from tourists.

Muliple choice

1 Before you listen, discuss these questions with your partner.

1 What are the benefits and drawbacks of tourism? Think about:

- mass tourism
- educational opportunities
- third-world economies
- employment opportunities
- the environment
- local cultures

2 How useful are guidebooks when you are travelling? What different types can you buy? What type would you choose?

2 You will hear an interview with Wendy Toller, author of a popular series of guidebooks used by backpackers and other independent travellers. For questions **1–6**, choose the answer **A**, **B**, **C** or **D** which you think fits best according to what you hear.

1 Wendy resents the suggestion that her guidebooks have

A exploited certain types of people.
B misled people about some things.
C succeeded for lack of competition.
D failed to provide realistic information.

2 Wendy admits that her guidebooks may

A persuade people to visit unsuitable places.
B fail to inform people of all dangers.
C give a negative impression of some places.
D influence people's choice of destination.

3 Through her guidebooks, Wendy hopes to make backpackers more

A patient with local people.
B informed about local agriculture.
C aware of the needs of local wildlife.
D respectful of the local way of life.

4 How does Wendy usually feel when she sees people using her guidebooks?

A worried
B indifferent
C relieved
D proud

5 What problem does Wendy see amongst some groups of young travellers today?

A a dependence on her guidebooks
B absence of a good reason for travelling
C shortage of new places to discover
D tendency to follow bad examples

6 How does Wendy feel about travel writing now?

A She views it from a purely business perspective.
B She's lost none of her original enthusiasm.
C She tries to avoid personal involvement.
D She's no longer interested in the travelling

PHRASAL VERBS 1 ▰▰▰▰▰▰▰▰▰▰▰▰▰▰▰▰▰▰▰▰▰▰▰▰▰▰▰▰▰▰▰▰▰▰▰

■ **1** Look at these two expressions used in the interview with Wendy Toller.

To make money out of someone.
To rip someone off.

■ **2** Look back at question 2.1 on page 185. Which word is closest in meaning to the expressions above?

■ **3** Are these two expressions synonyms? When would it be appropriate to use them?

■ **4** For questions **1–6**, write a new sentence as similar as possible in meaning to the original sentence but which uses one of the verbs from the box. You may need to change both the form of the verb and the structure of the sentence to do this.

discourage	decide	disappoint	exploit
persuade	enter	surrender	

Example: The agency was accused of ripping tourists off.

Answer: *The agency was accused of exploiting tourists.*

1 Mark's father tried to put him off the idea of travelling to Africa.

_____

2 I put great faith in Anthea, but I'm afraid in the end she let me down.

_____

3 David was keen to do the exam and put his name on the list.

_____

4 James talked his friends into joining him on a camping holiday.

_____

5 Diana hasn't made her mind up whether to go on holiday or not yet.

_____

6 After five years on the run, the escaped prisoner gave himself up to the police.

_____

■ **5** For questions **1–6**, write a new sentence as similar as possible in meaning to the original sentence but which uses one of the idiomatic expressions from the box in place of a verb.

to get on someone's nerves	get one's own back on someone
put a good word in for someone	to sort something out
make money out of someone	make a fool out of someone
make a mountain out of a molehill	

Example: Wendy was accused of exploiting penniless backpackers.

Answer: *Wendy was accused of making money out of penniless backpackers.*

1 John felt that his friends had been trying to humiliate him.

_____

2 After the argument, Sheila realized she had been exaggerating.

_____

3 Tony got the job because a rich uncle recommended him.

_____

4 William decided to take revenge on the man who'd cheated him.

_____

5 Don't invite Rosemary to the party, she really irritates me.

_____

6 I'm afraid my desk's in a dreadful mess; I need to reorganize everything.

_____

🎧 LISTENING 2
Matching

1 Before you listen, discuss these questions with your partner.

1 Is it better to go on holiday with family or friends? Why?

2 What are the advantages and disadvantages of going on holiday with a large group of people?

2 You will hear two colleagues, Lucy and Gary, talking about their friend's holiday plans. For questions **1–11**, decide which of the two speakers expresses each opinion. Write **L** for Lucy, **G** for Gary or **B** for both of them.

1 Rebecca's holiday sounds perfect.   **1** ☐

2 It is a good idea going on holiday in a large group.   **2** ☐

3 Rebecca may have been invited on the holiday for selfish reasons.   **3** ☐

4 It's a risk going on holiday with people you don't know.   **4** ☐

5 Rebecca's personality will help to make the holiday a success.   **5** ☐

6 Rebecca may find the holiday boring.   **6** ☐

7 There are likely to be tensions at the start of the holiday.   **7** ☐

8 There are bound to be arguments amongst the children.   **8** ☐

9 Rebecca may realize that this will be a different type of holiday for her.   **9** ☐

10 There are likely to be disagreements over travel arrangements.   **10** ☐

11 You have to admire Rebecca.   **11** ☐

SPEAKING 2
Describing places

1   Read these three passages which describe places. For each one, talk about:

- where you might expect to find it
- the intended audience
- the style
- the language used
- what you think about the points raised

Crystal waters meet white sand beaches fringed with palm trees. Its sub-tropical climate combined with breathtaking natural scenery and first class accommodation makes Mauritius ideal for those seeking rest and relaxation in the sun, with excellent sports facilities on hand. Mauritius also affords wonderful sightseeing, both naturally and culturally. Mist enshrouded volcanic peaks tower above sugar plantations, lush green forests and flower-filled villages that stretch down to the sea. The islanders themselves are friendly by nature, welcoming visitors with genuine enthusiasm.

Begun by George Vernon in 1661, Sudbury Hall is a monument to his ambition to make an impact on Restoration society. He created one of the most architecturally-intriguing houses of the time: it was built to a consciously outdated plan, yet George Vernon had his house sumptuously and fashionably decorated. The remarkable decoration includes carvings by Pierce and Grinling Gibbons, with superb plaster-work and decorative paintings by Laguerre.

It seems smaller, going back: the garden, the house, everything. But the garden especially. When I was a small child it was infinite: lawns, paths, high hedges, the rose garden, the long reach of the kitchen garden, the spinney with the silver birches. It was a completed world; beyond lay nothingness. In fact, now, I see a landscape of fields and hills and lanes, tranquil and harmless – but then it was the unpredictable, into which one did not go. We turned back at the gates. These defined our world: the safe, controlled world of the garden.

2   Choose two of the passages and compare them using the points in question 1.

WRITING 1
Describing a place

1 Read this composition title.

Describe a place that you know well that has been changed or may be changed by tourism, saying whether you think the changes have been or will be for the better or not.

2 Make notes under the following headings.

1 Description of the place:
   • facts
   • my feelings about it

2 What it was like before/What it is like now?

3 What happened/may happen to change it?

4 Why the changes have happened/will happen?
   • prospects for the future/my opinions

3 Tell your partner about the place you are planning to write about. Use your notes to help you.

4 Use your notes to make a plan for your composition, then write it. Write no more than 350 words.

USE OF ENGLISH 1
Cloze passage

1 What do you know about the Hawaiian islands? What type of holiday do you think people have there?

2 Fill each of the numbered blanks in the passage with **one** suitable word.

How I lied my way to the top

The man from *Rent-a-Car* in Hawaii must have read adventure books as a child; (**1**) _____ final words as he (**2**) _____ over the keys to the four-wheeled drive vehicle provided a perfect dare. 'Don't go on the Saddle Road, ' he said.

I was on Big Island, the largest and (**3**) _____ southerly of the Hawaiian chain. There are two dormant volcanoes on the island and between them (**4**) _____ the Saddle Road a bumpy, remote and rather frightening route that (**5**) _____ the island from east to west.

One (**6**) _____ why the car-hire companies are scared (**7**) _____ this thin, winding piece of rutted tarmac may be that its fifty-mile length is (**8**) _____ isolated and high that if you (**9**) _____ down, it would be difficult to tow you (**10**) _____ . Another perhaps is that the US military (**11**) _____ use of the desolate landscape through (**12**) _____ the road passes; mass tourism might spoil the war games.

Yet another reason is that a spur road off the Saddle leads to the very top of Mauna Kea, and (**13**) _____ signs warn you not to, it is awfully tempting to swing the wheel over at this point and (**14**) _____ a go. I had two reasons for (**15**) _____ so, one of which was simply that Mauna Kea is taller than Mount Everest, (**16**) _____ for the fact that its base is actually under water, and (**17**) _____ the summit are some of the world's finest telescopes.

So, I lied, took the keys and headed (**18**) _____ the Saddle Road. As I (**19**) _____ off, the beaches were bathed (**20**) _____ warm sunshine. Yet on top of Mauna Kea, maybe two hour's drive away, I could see snow

3 What is a dare? (line 3) Tell your partner about a time when you did something as a dare.

READING 2

Multiple choice

1 What do you understand by the term stress?

- what are the symptoms?
- who suffers from it?
- what causes it?
- how can it be remedied?

2 Read the passage about stress carefully.

Stress what stress?

More than half the adult population claims to be suffering from it. From victims of rising crime to exhausted working mothers, from tightly-squeezed professionals to the despairing unemployed. It makes us tense, irritable and affects our concentration . Worse, it damages our health, causing everything from heart attacks to asthma, from
10 *chronic fatigue to spots.*

Cynics are quick to dismiss the phenomenon as fashionable hype. And they have a point. After all, we are living longer lives than any generation before us. Most of us have more cash, more holidays, more consumer durables, and more choices in our lives than ever before. Faced with the historical evidence of human survival, triumph and even happiness, against far greater odds than we experience today, talk of stress, the modern disease,
20 just sounds like whingeing. Yet for many people stress is real enough. The effects of sudden and shocking events on physical and mental health have been well documented. But, crises are not the only things to damage our health. Professor Ben Fletcher, psychologist and Dean of the Business School at the University of Hertfordshire, argues that the work people do has a huge effect on their risk of physical disease. High demands, combined with low control, lack of support, and especially monotonous work, are
30 stressful and increase our chances of an early death.

The evidence is persuasive. Danish bus drivers who faced the worst traffic lived shorter lives than colleagues on quiet country roads. Meanwhile, civil servants who feared unemployment during reorganization, were more likely to report health problems than more secure colleagues. And the unemployed – those with most boredom, least control over their lives, and greatest anxiety about finding new work – are more likely than any other
40 group to commit suicide.

But does it make sense to sweep all these conditions under one title, 'stress'? The boredom of the unemployed is very different from the frustration of the bus driver, and the grief of the recently bereaved. Yet professionals, as well as the general public, persist in using the term. According to Carry Cooper, Professor of Organizational Psychology at the University of Manchester, it's an umbrella concept. While cause, context and response all vary, the
50 underlying model is the same. Hans Selye, founder of modern research into stress, described it as ' the rate of wear and tear on the body'. The analogy emerges out of physics. Subject a bridge to repeated stress – perhaps the waves against the pillars, or steady vibrations from soldiers marching across it in step – and it will start to exhibit strain.

But stress is not entirely malign. A certain amount of pressure – Professor Cooper distinguishes pressure from stress – and we thrive. We keep going, we keep
60 interested in the world, we stay alive. Too much and we get tense, troubled, breathless and run down. For example, the hormones produced by the 'fight and flight' mechanism – including adrenaline – while

inspiring us to react properly to crises, can also damage our bodies. All it takes is one final stressful straw and the camel's back will crack.

Of course, it will crack in different ways depending on the form of stress we are exposed to, our own genetic make up and the support we have to help us
70 cope. Personality matters too – even if scientists can't quite agree about which personality traits are at fault and why. In the late sixties, Dr Freidman and Dr Rosenman claimed that aggressive extrovert achievers were more likely to die of a heart attack than calmer people. Now the pendulum has swung the other way. Research reported in a recent edition of the *Lancet* shows that people who bottle up their emotions are more likely to die early, and in particular to have heart attacks.

80 So stress is real. The answer to our cynics who point to historical evidence is that our ancestors suffered from stress too. Richard Napier, a sixteenth century physician, recorded that around a third of his patients were 'troubled in the mind'. As psychologist, Dr Anthony Clare points out, this is almost exactly the same as the proportion of visitors at today's doctor's surgery who are recorded as experiencing stress-related problems. We are no more wimpish than our forebears, the stress they suffered probably
90 contributing to their ill health and lower life expectancy.

Of course the stresses we face today are different – and may genuinely be greater for many people than thirty years ago. Compared with the Fifties and Sixties, we are all working far longer hours. The middle classes in particular are having to compete, where in the past their positions were guaranteed. Professor Cooper argues that we have less support today to help us deal with the inevitable stresses that
100 arise. We no longer have the communities and extended families that acted as natural sources of moral support. So counselling networks and services have had to grow in their place. But the big test is to whether our futures will be consistently more stressful than our past, how will human beings manage to adapt to change? As we move from one job to another, acquiring new skills, meeting new people, we will always have to cope with constant fluidity in our lives. Will this always be tough to cope
110 with or will the next generation, brought up on a diet of rapid movement, get used to continual change? No one knows, but the academics look forward to finding out.

3 Now answer the questions **1–7**. Choose the answer **A**, **B**, **C** or **D** which you think fits best.

1 What is suggested by the 'cynics'?

   A Stress results from too many choices.
   B There is no historical evidence for stress.
   C As people live longer, so stress increases.
   D People always find something to complain about.

2 Ben Fletcher points out that stress

   A often follows traumatic events.
   B may be connected with boredom.
   C is a purely physical condition.
   D can result from other illnesses.

3 Professor Cooper thinks that stress

   A is overused as a term.
   B has its basis in positive responses.
   C is an aspect of personality.
   D has parallels in the physical world.

4 Contemporary theories discount the link between high levels of stress and

   A aggressive behaviour.
   B heart disease.
   C emotion.
   D personality.

5 The evidence of Richard Napier supports the idea that, in the past, people

   A used different terminology.
   B were also cynical about stress.
   C had similar symptoms to today.
   D suffered more acutely from stress.

6 Professor Cooper connects modern stress-related problems to a lack of

   A personal flexibility.
   B financial security.
   C social stability.
   D professional support.

7 Which word best describes the writer's general attitude towards the ideas put forward by those who study stress?

   A sceptical
   B receptive
   C indifferent
   D dismissive

VOCABULARY 1
Definitions

1 Explain each of the following words and expressions from the passage, in your own words.

1 consumer durables (line 15)
2 far greater odds (line 18)
3 whingeing (line 20)
4 well-documented (lines 22–23)
5 analogy (line 52)
6 run down (line 61)
7 the final straw (lines 65–66)
8 traits (line 71)
9 bottle up (line 77)
10 wimpish (line 88)
11 moral support (line 102)
12 fluidity (line 109)

USE OF ENGLISH 2
Noun phrases

1

1 Which two words in paragraph one of the passage on stress are joined by a hyphen?

2 Why has this type of punctuation been used?

3 Can you find another example of its use in the passage?

2 Rewrite each of these sentences so that it includes a hyphenated noun phrase.

1 I am in favour of measures which cut costs.

2 This new deal will secure the prospects of the company in the long term.

3 The company employed some consultants who are paid extremely highly.

4 The plant grows best on slopes which face North.

5 The tournament is held every four years.

6 Production increased thanks to the introduction of machinery which allowed less labour to be used.

7 He has no difficulty in motivating himself.

8 The business is regarded as quite a small scale affair.

9 I bought the pullover from a company that sells via mail order.

10 The company called in an accountant with very good qualifications.

SPEAKING 3
Talking about photographs

A

B

1 Choose one of the two pictures labelled **A** and **B**. Think about the cultural aspects of your picture. Look at the other picture. Think of some questions to ask your partner about the cultural aspects of their picture.

1 Talk about your picture with your partner. What comparisons or contrasts can you make between the two pictures?

2 Talk about one of the following topics, use the ideas below to help you.

It's a small world and it's getting smaller every day.

Do you agree with this comment? Talk about:

- preserving cultural differences
- role of international companies
- development of technology
- population growth
- language barriers
- solving global problems
- avoiding conflict

2 To what extent do you think modern life is more stressful than life was hundreds of years ago? Talk about:

work and leisure	pace of life
poverty, famine, drought	working hours
speed of communications	disease and working expectancy
social pressures	role of education and qualifications

In the speaking test, REMEMBER:

- say what you think, don't wait to be asked;
- make the conversation interesting for the examiner;
- try to speak naturally, talk to the examiner, not to the picture or text;
- try to develop the topic by introducing new ideas;
- smile, try not to look too nervous!

WRITING 2
Choosing your composition

1 Imagine that you are in the exam. Read these composition titles. Which two titles would you choose? Why?

1 Write a story beginning with these words.

Looking back, I'm really embarrassed by the way I behaved that day. It all began ...

2 An international company plans to open a new fast-food restaurant in the historic centre of a famous city in your country.

Write a letter to the local newspaper either

a in support of the proposal saying why such a development is needed

OR

b objecting to the proposal, saying why such a development would be inappropriate.

3 This advertisement has appeared in a magazine for English language students. You are interested in taking part in the project and receiving some advice. Write to the company.

LEARN ENGLISH FREE!

English language students wanted to try out new computer software designed to help you brush up your language skills.

If you are interested, write telling us your level of English, your access to hardware and why you think you are the right person to take part in the project.

We also offer free advice to internet users, and those thinking of investing in hardware and software.

Ask for details if interested.

Write to: Compupals, P.O. box 27, London.

4 *Stress does not really exist as a medical condition it is just an attitude of mind.'* To what extent do you agree with this statement? Write an article for a newspaper either agreeing or disagreeing with the statement.

5 Your English-speaking pen-friend has asked you to recommend a book to read over the summer holidays. Write a letter to your friend recommending a book you have read recently, saying why you think it would be suitable.

2 Make plans for the titles you have chosen. Write down your ideas in note form. Did you make a good choice?

Remember

No one type of composition is easier than the other. It is important to read all the questions carefully before deciding. It is useful to underline the main points in the question to remind yourself to include them. Choose the questions which YOU can write about most easily.

Don't forget to:

- make good use of time; you need to allow time for:
  - choosing
  - planning
  - writing
  - checking

- make a plan and notes of the content

- make sure your answer is relevant

- make sure you cover all points

- think about the examiner

- make your writing interesting

- write clearly

EXAM PRACTICE 10

1 In this section, you must choose the word or phrases, **A**, **B**, **C** or **D** which best completes each sentence.

1 Academics _____ in using the term stress to describe a variety of conditions.

    A continue   **B** insist   **C** persist   **D** endure

2 Backpackers tend to have an accepted _____ of dress.

    A code   **B** norm   **C** fashion   **D** style

3 For a backpacker, carrying a suitcase would be like _____ social suicide.

    A enacting   **B** committing   **C** executing   **D** composing

4 Ray didn't want to _____ attention to the fact that he was consulting a guidebook.

    A pull   **B** take   **C** draw   **D** raise

5 Backpackers may _____ down upon people who don't follow their conventions.

    A glance   **B** look   **C** view   **D** glare

6 I need to do a course to _____ up my keyboard skills, I'm a bit rusty.

    A dust   **B** shine   **C** rub   **D** brush

7 The islander are, _____ nature, very friendly.

    A at   **B** of   **C** by   **D** from

8 There's no point insisting, Glenda won't be _____ into doing anything she doesn't want to do.

    A talked   **B** reasoned   **C** convinced   **D** chatted

9 Lucy suspected the holiday families of inviting Rebecca for ulterior _____.

    A purposes   **B** motives   **C** objectives   **D** intentions

10 Danny resolved to _____ his own back for the trick played on him.

    A get   **B** have   **C** take   **D** hold

2 Fill each of the numbered spaces in the passage with **one** suitable word.

Caravan holidays

Caravanning must be one of the great inscrutable mysteries of modern British life. There are around 600,000 caravans of various (**1**) _____ and sizes in the UK and in the (**2**) _____ o 60 million holiday nights each year are spent in (**3**) _____ .

But what is it that makes people want to set (**4**) _____ a bonsai version of their home, complete with all the trappings (**5**) _____ modern life and trundle it around the country (**6**) _____ wheels? Most caravanners (**7**) _____ off with a tent and slowly (**8**) _____ upwards through various small caravans that have to be towed behind a car. These they equip with (**9**) _____ manner of space-saving gadgetry to provide the perfect home from home (**10**) _____ miniature. Eventually, they may even (**11**) _____ the stage of buying the ultimate luxury, an American-style camper van, a motorized caravan (**12**) _____ almost much space inside as a real home.

Psychologist, Oliver James points (**13**) _____ the proverb, 'an Englishman's home is his castle' to (**14**) _____ the phenomenon of caravanning. The castle, he says, is the perfect metaphor (**15**) _____ the British personality, a fortress within (**16**) _____ people's innermost thoughts and feelings remain concealed (**17**) _____ others.

There remains, however, a basic need to (**18**) _____ the human instinct to mingle in public places, to socialize. The caravan provides an ideal solution to this dilemma (**19**) _____ allowing people to combine both anti-social and social instincts. When an Englishman engages in recreation, therefore, he does his (**20**) _____ to take his castle with him.

3 Fill each of the blanks with a suitable word or phrase.

1 When he complained, John was told that the fault on his computer was due to normal _____ tear.

2 After so many disappointments, the cancellation of the concert was _____ straw for Debbie.

3 The investigation showed that the accident may have _____ of a mechanical fault.

4 After two years' travelling, Marta felt she'd finally got the travel bug _____ system.

5 Tom's full of vitality, he's the _____ soul of the party.

6 You have to admire Tessa; whatever the challenge, she's willing _____ a go.

4 For each of the sentences below, write a new sentence as similar as possible in meaning to the original sentence, but using the word given. This word **must not be altered** in any way.

Example: A lot of people attended the meeting.

turnout

Answer: *There was a very good turnout for the meeting.*

1 Everyone has a great deal of respect for Mr Jones the accountant.
highly

2 The kids will be so excited after the journey, arguments will be inevitable.
bound

3 I only have to think of all those children and I get a headache.
thought

4 It doesn't matter how old people are, they can still join the youth club.
regardless

5 The demand for guidebooks has been rising steadily this year.
rise

6 For some reason, we never considered the possibility of renting a car in Hawaii.

occurred

7 The plane is already one hour behind schedule and it hasn't taken off yet.
due

8 A serious earthquake destroyed our hopes of spending a month travelling in the area.
paid

9 Penny couldn't find anything interesting for the little boy to do while he waited.
loss

10 People have been saying that some of the details those guidebooks were invented
alleged

5 Finish each of the following sentences in such a way that it is as similar as possible in meaning to the sentence printed before it.

Example: Immediately after his departure things improved.

Answer: No sooner *had he departed than things improved.*

1 Given continued good weather, we should arrive in Sydney by Thursday.

Provided _____

2 I had only just started opening the parcel when the phone rang.

Hardly _____

3 Jonathan didn't feel angry; actually he was quite pleased.

Far _____

4 We will repaint the house in time for your visit next year.

By the _____

5 Immediately after Graham had gone, Pauline put on her coat and went out.

No sooner _____

6 Only by booking a seat in advance can you be sure to see the match.

Unless _____

7 Although the plant looks nice, its berries are deadly poisonous.

Nice _____

8 I ought to warn Mrs Fellows about the train strike, ' thought Dennis.

Dennis thought he'd _____

9 'Please, please, don't tell my mother what you've seen,' Marie said to Darren.

Marie pleaded _____

10 Although it seemed trivial at the time, Denise wished she'd reported the incident to the police.

Trivial _____

Help with writing

■1 When the examiners read the compositions you write in the exam, they award a mark out of 20 for each composition. The examiners are looking for these things in the compositions:

Task realization. Each of the question types asks for a different type of writing laid out in the appropriate way. What you say in your composition has to be relevant to the question and must communicate your ideas clearly. If you are asked to write a letter, for example, it must look like a letter and follow certain conventions such as, correct opening and closing phrases etc. If you asked to write an article, on the other hand, it will be laid out differently and written in a different style.

Organization. The division of the composition into sentences and paragraphs and how these are linked together are important aspects to consider. A composition which is badly organized is difficult to read and may not communicate the intended ideas successfully.

Range of vocabulary and structure. The examiners will be looking for evidence that you can write in English using a good range of grammatical structures and vocabulary in an accurate way. Correct spelling and punctuation are also important and the workbook has exercises to give you extra help in these areas.

Length. The examination questions tell you how many words to write. If you write too little, then you will lose some of the marks. If you write too much, then only the first part of your composition will be assessed. However, it is not a good idea to waste too much time in the exam counting the words. Practise timing your compositions when you are preparing so that you get a feel for what is the right length of answer and how best to organize your time.

Handwriting. Poor handwriting, spelling errors and faulty punctuation are not specifically penalised. But the examiners will reduce the mark if these areas are so bad that they make it difficult to understand what has been written.

Irrelevance. Remember you get no marks if you introduce material you have learnt by heart and which is not relevant to the question. You can only pass the exam by answering the questions set with your own ideas expressed in your own words.

■2 Look at these compositions written by students preparing to take the Proficiency examination. For each one decide whether:

- the question has been answered satisfactorily;
- the writing has been well organized;
- the style of writing is appropriate;
- the layout is appropriate;
- there is a good range of grammar and vocabulary;
- all parts are relevant and clear;
- the length is acceptable;
- the errors prevent us understanding what is written.

What mark out of twenty would you give each composition?

N.B. These are real students' compositions which contain errors. They are not models for you to copy.

When you have thought about the compositions, read the examiner's mark and comments.

The question which the three students have chosen is:

Write a story beginning with these words.

> *Helen closed the door behind her and let out a deep sigh.*
> *What a day it had been ....*

Helen closed the door behind her and let out a deep sigh. What a day it had been, fighting with the powers of nature but with her powers too. But let's take it from the beginning.

It was a beautiful, sunny day, so Helen decided to take the bust and go visit her cousins who were living in a small town, 80 klm far from her home. She prepared and went to the bus station and waited. After half an hour she was on her way to her cousin's home. As the trip was very tiring the bus made a stop in the middle of a forest so that the passengers would relax and take some fresh air. Amazed by the sound of birds singing, a little river flowing and leaves rustling due to the breeze, Helen started walking through the forest, enjoying its magic.

Suddenly she realized that she had gone far away from the bus. She panicked and started calling for help and trying to find from which path did she get there. Bus as she was looking for the part, she moved deeper in the forest and got lost for good. The night was coming and she was alone among strange animals and plants. With the first drop on her head she knew that a storm was about to come and she had to find a haven. Finally she found a cave and decided to stay there for the rest of the night. Meanwhile her parents and cousins who were informed of her trip, started worrying and called the police to search for her.

The other day, the rain had stopped and the sun raised in the sky. Helen felt afraid and alone. She went out to find any fruits to eat. But suddenly she heard people calling her name. She knew that her little odyssey was over. After a few hours she was back to her home, in her room, thinking of the adventure she had.

COMPOSITION 1

This is a weak narrative composition. 'let's take it from the beginning' is a good way to start, but there is not much more in the way of narrative style. The sequence of tenses is not always quite appropriate (e.g. past simple/past perfect) and the time references are sometimes confusing (e.g. 'the other day').

The language is careful and easy to understand, but very limited in range. There are also a number of basic errors of both grammar (e.g. 'from which path did she get there', 'any fruits') and vocabulary (e.g. 'Helen decided to take the bust' and 'Bus as she was looking for the part') which could lead to confusion.

This piece of writing is not at Proficiency standard and gets a mark of 8/20.

Helen closed the door behind her and let out a deep sigh. What a day it had been for her. She had been busy all day long with the arrangements and the demands of her wedding. She had woken up at seven o'clock so that to take care of everything that she needed for the most beautiful day of her life which was finally approaching with the pass of the time.

First of all she went to the jeweler's shop with her fiance Chris, to choose their wedding rings. It was very difficult for her to choose between so many expensive and dazzling jewels. But with the help of the shop assistant and mostly her fiance she managed to make her choice and she really did, she loved their wedding rings. After that, she had to be at nine o'clock to the department store with the wedding waves and equipment because she had an appointment with the dressmakers for her wedding dress and for her bridesmaids gowns who were there waiting for her. When she arrived she saw her friend and told them how happy she was that all the people she loved were with her in the most important and beautiful time of her whole life! She was very thrilled and excited but anxious too, because she had so many things to do and so many obligations to fulfill today. She wore the dress which was very elegant and beautiful. She was looking very charming and stunning with her wedding dress. She looked as the most beautiful woman in the world. In the same way were her bridesmaids also been dressed.

Right after that she went to the other floor of the store to make some arrangements for the decorations of the church and for the sugar almonds and particularly for the established wedding cake. She had to decide for the color, for their form, for their quality. She had to decide about everything. When she had finished with that she decided to rest for a short time because she had been very tired and hungry too.

When she had a rest she drove to the typography of her best friend Nataly who had expecting her there at two o'clock to decide for the wedding invitations. Helen had a great difficulty in choosing what form of invitation she would take. Her best friend and her best woman helped her a lot to decide quickly and effectively and took the most specatcular, romantic invitations. When she finished with that she had one more task to take care of before calling it a day. She had to go to rent a big and luxurious limousine. That limousine was supposed to lead her to the church and to her beloved future husband. It didn't take her too long to take care of that task and she finished with that rather quickly.

It was half past four when she last saw the time while she was driving back to her house. Thank God she had taken care of a lot of obligations and now she wasn't feeling so anxious and drained for her wedding. But even if she was very tired she felt very happy and amused for her wedding day which was going to be the most gorgeous and terrific wedding of the world!

COMPOSITION 2

This is a better attempt at a narrative. It is well organized and follows on well from the opening. The sequence of events is clear and the writer manages to convey Helen's feelings successfully.

The language is natural and fluent, despite a number of errors (e.g. 'she had been very tired' 'In the same way were her bridesmaids also been dressed'). The sentence structure, although rather simple, is generally good, despite inconsistent use of the past simple and past perfect tenses. Some inappropriate vocabulary choices cause occasional problems for the reader (e.g. wedding waves, the typography).

This is a borderline piece of writing at Proficiency level and gets a mark of 11/20.

Helen closed the door behind her and let out a deep sigh. What a day it had been. She crossed the room and threw herself heavily on the couch, closed her eyes and played the whole day back in her mind.

That morning Helen had been woken up by the telephone ringing at an early hour, at least that was what she thought at first.

She opened her eyes, got out of bed and stumbled over some books which were lying nearby. She fell, swore loudly and got up again, run through the hall and literally jumped over the telephone.

When she answered, the voice at the other end shouting her name said 'Are you crazy? It's 09:10. The exam is on at 10:00. What are you still doing at home?' It was Iaia, her classmate from her English course. They were supposed to meet up at 08:45 that morning, to have a cup of coffee together and most importantly, to calm each other down before the examination. Realising the mess she was in, Helen reassured Iaia and told her she would see her at the college. She hung up and went straight to the bathroom. She washed her face, brushed her teeth, grabbed the first clothes she saw and dressed as quickly as possible. Helen then flew out of the house and run to the tube station to be faced with a 20 minute journey.

She couldn't believe what had happened. She was extremely agitated and started panicing. On top of everything else, she remembered she had sworn. The Egyptian proverb: "To curse in the morning is to curse the whole day", started echoing in her mind.

When Helen arrived at the college it was 10:10. She went to the examination room and to her horror the door was closed. After a moment of hesitation, Helen opened the door. The examiners were distributing the exam papers. Feeling extremely embarrassed, she apologised and explained the reason for her delay. She was convinced they would ask her to leave, but to her surprise they allowed her in. She went to the first available desk she saw and sat down.

Helen turned the paper over. She had to write an essay of 800 words choosing from four headings. She looked down the titles and chose number three: What is courage?: She took a few deep breaths and simply wrote: This is courage: _____, then put the pen down and sat back.

When the examiners announced that the time was over, without even looking for Iaia, Helen went home.

COMPOSITION 3

This is a good narrative composition that is slightly above the word limit indicated.

The task is reasonably well achieved with a competent description of a sequence of events that is clear and easy to follow. The paragraphing is appropriate to the story, which shows evidence of good planning.

The language is almost completely free of errors, although 'run' for ran occurs twice, indicating that this may be more than just a slip of the pen. The use of prepositions is not completely accurate and there are some spelling mistakes, but the meaning is always clear.

The range of structure and vocabulary is adequate for dealing with a story about everyday events and the writer has adopted a consistent style that shows good awareness of the target reader.

This is a competent piece of writing at Proficiency level that gets a mark of 15/20.

Macmillan Heinemann English Language Teaching
Macmillan Oxford, Between Towns Road, Oxford OX4 2PP
A division of Macmillan Publishers Limited

Companies and representatives throughout the world

ISBN 0 435 24520 1

Text © Nick Kenny 1999
Design and illustration © Macmillan Publishers Limited 1999
Heinemann is a registered trademark of Reed Educational and Professional Publishing Limited

First published 1999

Designed by Glynis Edwards
Illustrated by: Paul Beebee, Hardlines, Kath Walker

Acknowledgements
The author would like to thank Nikos Demenopoulos, Jill Florent, Cristina Forosetto, Lynn Gold, Jean Kennedy, Barbara Lewis, Clive Nightingale, Sotiria Vamvakidou and Ian Tolley for their help and advice. Special thanks to my editor Sarah Curtis and to Emma Parker for researching the photographs.

The author and publishers would like to thank the following for permission to reproduce copyright material:
Jonathan Blezard for an extract from *Garden Bird News*, p162; Lucinda Bredin for the articles 'Shaggy Dog Story' (*The Independent*, 24.8.96), pp30–31; and 'How to live with your own Cezanne' (*The Sunday Telegraph Review*, 11.2.96), pp124–125; Cambridge University Press for an extract from *The Cambridge Encyclopaedia of Language* ©1987 by David Crystal, p55 and extracts from *Working with Words: A Guide to Teaching and Learning Vocabulary* ©1986 by Ruth Gairns and Stuart Redman, p108, p110 and p119; *Cambridgeshire Journal* for a 'Wedding Car' extract, p93 and an extract by Dr Peter Rowan, p73; Curtis Brown Group Ltd on behalf of the Estate of S.T. Haymon for an extract from *The Quivering Tree* ©1990 by Sylvia Haymon, pp64–65; Eaglemoss Publications Ltd for an extract from *Find Out More Magazine* 1996, p142; Egmont Children's Books for an extract from *Going Back* by Penelope Lively, p188; Express Newspapers Ltd for extracts from articles 'Deep-fried coronary' by Jonathan Miller (*Sunday Express Magazine*, 25.8 96), p19; an item by John Ingham (*The Express*, 4.3.97), p33; 'On the Lilo' by Oliver James (*Sunday Express Magazine*, 25.2.96), p68; 'Does Mummy know best?' by India Knight (*Sunday Express Magazine*, 3.3.96), pp166–167; Future Publishing Ltd for extracts from Classic CD Magazine, pp88–89 and p94; Guardian Media Group for extracts from articles 'Suspect is blue, large and hairy' by Martin Wainright (*The Guardian*, 16.4.96), p33; 'Daughter of the Iron House' (*The Guardian* 11.3.96), p138; 'Bohemia hosts alienated tribe' by William Booth (*The Guardian*, 12.3.96), p152; 'Blowing the Mortgage at Monte Carlo' by Paul Kelso (*The Guardian*, 16.9.96), p175; Sue Hallam for the article 'Does music make you sharp?' (*Daily Telegraph*, 28.2.96), p98 ;Independent Newspapers for the articles 'Crisis in a sesame seed bun' by Paul Vallely (*The Independent*, 27.3.96), pp2–3; 'Supermarket sweep' by John Hind (*The Independent*, 18.1.97), p8; 'Afraid to open wide' by Sandra Alexander (*The Independent*, 17.9.96), pp12–13; 'One of my pet hates' by David Aaronovitch (*The Independent*, 24.8.96), pp22–23; 'The joy of reading leaves men on the shelf' by Marianne MacDonald and Michael Streeter (*The Independent*, 2.1.97), p51; 'They don't make them like they used to' by Dominic Lutyens (*The Independent Weekend*, 9.3.96), p84; 'Action replay' by Jim White (*The Independent Magazine*, 4.5.96), p158; 'Who loves the firm today?' by Jack O'Sullivan (*The Independent*, 8.8.96), pp171–172; 'A sticky business' by Rosalinde Sharpe (*The Independent Magazine*, 20.4.96), p178; 'Stress? It's as old as the hills' by Yvette Cooper (*The Independent*, 8.5.96), pp190–191;

'Miles Tea: the best drink of the holiday' by Mike Prestage (*The Independent* 24.8.96), p170; Lands' End Direct Merchants UK for an extract from their catalogue, p163; Ewan MacNaughton Associates on behalf of the Telegraph Group Ltd for articles by Robert Matthews (*Sunday Telegraph*, 14.4.96), p104 and John McEwen (*Sunday Telegraph*, 10.3.96), p129; Paul Mansfield for his article 'Not the done thing – backpacking' (*Sunday Telegraph*, 21.4.96) pp182–183; The National Magazine Company Ltd for the article 'A few words on kitchen towels' (*Esquire Magazine*, October 1995) p134; The National Trust for an extract from the guidebook to Sudbury Hall, p188; New Scientist for the article 'Strolling by numbers' by Helen Muir (*New Scientist*, 5.7.97), p151 and two job advertisements (*New Scientist*, 20.9.97), p162 and p163; Penguin Books Ltd for the cover illustration of *Next to Nature, Art*, p131; Random House UK Ltd for an extract from *Next to Nature, Art* by Penelope Lively, pp130–131; Nicholas Roe for his article 'How I lied my way to the top' (*Sunday Telegraph*, 24.3.96), p189; Steven Rose for an extract from *The Making of Memory* ©1992, p146; Royal Doulton plc for an extract from 'Lawleys by Post' advertising campaign, p93; The Society of Authors for an extract from the article 'Reaching out' by Derek Parker (*The Author*, Spring 1998), p58; Times Newspapers Limited for extracts from the article Generation gap: reading other people's letters' by Candida Crewe (*The Times Magazine*, 13.6.98), ©Times Newspapers Limited 1999, p153; R. Twining & Co Ltd for extracts from a publicity leaflet, pp27–29; Keith Waterhouse for his article 'I hate holidays', p79

The author and publishers would like to thank the following for permission to reproduce their photographs:
Abode p135(t); The Advertising Archives p143(tl, bl & br); Allsport/Ross Kinnaird p148; Ancient Art & Architecture/ Ronald Sheridan p114; Arcaid/Nicholas Kane p135(b); © Jason Bell/The Sunday Times, London p149(b); Anthony Blake Photo Library p1(ml & mr); Gareth Bowden/©MHELT p1(t & bl); © Joel Chant/Newsteam p121(ml); Corbis UK p141; Haddon Davies/©MHELT p1(br); Mary Evans Picture Library p35; Paul Freestone/©MHELT p46(t); Ronald Grant Archive pp81, 82, 85, 86; Chris Honeywell/Working Images p61(br); Chris Honeywell/ ©MHELT p52; Image Bank p13; Images Colour Library p61(t); Impact Photos pp(© Peter Menzel/Material World)106, (© Peter Ginter/Material World)107, (Mark Cator)149(t), (Alexis Waller- stein)151, (Piers Cavendish)161(bl), (Peter Arkell)181(tl), (John Cole)181(br), (Caroline Penn)183; Jeremy Friers p61(bl); D.J. Miles & Co. p170; A.Painter p129; Performing Arts Library pp89, 90, 91; © Tom Pilston/The Independent p121(b); Popperfoto pp6(b), 33, 51; Frank Spooner (©Godlewski/Liaison) p21(b), (©Keister/Liaison) p26; Superstock Ltd (Chen, Tsing-Fang, *The Awakening Gypsy*) p127(r), (Derain, André, *Harbour of Westminster* ©ADAGP, Paris & DACS, London 1999) p127(tl), (Mondrian, Piet *Tableau No. 1* ©1999 Mondrian/Holtzman Trust c/o Beeldrecht, Amsterdam, Holland & DACS, London) p127(bl); Tony Stone Images pp6(t), 21(mr), 46(b), 69, 101(b), 161(tr & mr), 181(tr & bl), 188, 190, 193(r); © Edward Sykes/The Independent p101(t); Topham Picturepoint pp(PA)21(t), 21(ml), (PA)62, 121(tl), (UNEP/Nicolette Marsella)193(l); Varig Airlines/ ©MHELT p161(br); World Pictures p121(tr).

Commissioned photography by: Chris Honeywell p143(tr) and p175.

Printed and bound in Spain by Mateu Cromo SA

2003 2002 2001 2000 1999
10 9 8 7 6 5 4 3 2 1